ELMER'S TRIBAL WAR

ELMER'S TRIBAL WAR

RICHARD ALUMBAUGH

Boyle
&
Dalton

Book Design & Production
Columbus Publishing Lab
www.ColumbusPublishingLab.com

Paperback ISBN: 978-1-63337-263-4
E-book ISBN: 978-1-63337-264-1

Printed in the United States of America
1 3 5 7 9 10 8 6 4 2

In memory of my loving wife, Jo Anne.

Prologue

I had put our Pacific oceanside home up for sale. Jo Anne, my wife, had succumbed to small cell cancer on May 29, 2003. A year had passed. I was ready to move on from grieving. I gave away or recycled her personal belongings.

Rummaging through one of the judicial files Jo Anne left behind, I came upon the case of a father and son who had been tried for murder. The defendants and victim were enrollees of the Colville Federation of Tribes. Thumbing through the transcripts of the trial brought back memories. In the early morning hours of August 27, 1986, a skirmish resembling a war firefight erupted as police approached a chicken coop where the father, Elmer McGinnis and his son, Patrick Hoffman, were hidden. A tribal police officer was killed and another seriously wounded. My story begins prior to the shoot-out with Elmer McGinnis contacting his attorney, William Cottrell. For Elmer, tribal corruption had to be stopped.

Chapter 1

Restless

William Cottrell, a district court judge and part-time attorney in Omak, Washington, was not surprised that Elmer McGinnis dropped by his small office. Elmer and his attorney had a long-standing professional and personal relationship.

Elmer came right to the point. "I'm not about to let those goddamned councilmen and their goons on the police force take us out. They got a contract on me and my son." Elmer pressed further. "The council has done it before and would do it again. They've got a contract on us because we know too much about their damn corruption. A hell of a lot of money has passed under the table from outsiders to steal our minerals and our timber. They have stonewalled me on rights to my allotment going back to my grandfather. The council is up to their eyeballs in payoffs protecting these land deals."

His attorney had heard these complaints before, but Elmer was undeterred. "I've got the original deed to show John McGinnis's name is on that deed signed by the Department of the Interior." Elmer and other Colville enrollees who had filed allotment claims were frustrated by the lack of progress. Navigating the complex maze of federal law to resolve claims disputes proved difficult and, for many, too expensive.

Cottrell listened patiently. He knew the McGinnis family well, and was a gun collector like Elmer and his son Patrick. Elmer had been his client since he first represented Elmer's younger son, James, who was arrested for drug possession in 1981.

"I will protect my family, whatever it takes," Elmer said with a tremor in his voice. His shaky hands and speech likely had something to do with a tree hitting him or a stroke. No one seemed to know precisely the cause.

Cottrell had been a buffer for Elmer. When James was arrested as a teenager and convicted for drug possession, Cottrell took possession of Elmer's extensive gun collection as a condition for James's reduced sentence and parole. That was five years ago. James had since settled down and married.

Elmer pressed his attorney about the council's denial of enrollment for his daughters to become members of the Colville Confederation of Tribes. "Dale Kohler is on the take, and he knows I'm on to him," Elmer said forcefully. "Denying my daughters enrollment is payback."

Cottrell listened without comment on the allegations. "I'll call Dale Kohler and see if we can't get this enrollment problem settled."

"You won't get anywhere with him," Elmer said. "They're all in it together. Look what happened to Bobby Jo Covington. The tribal police took him out. That story that Bobby was drunk and missed a curve going home from the War Bonnet is bullshit. Bobby was on the wagon and never touched a drink that night. It's as plain as God made little green apples—the cops followed him and forced him off the road.

"My son knows who did it. It was Lou Millard," Elmer added. "Millard's police car had dents in the front and paint smears that matched paint on Bobby's motorcycle. It was all about Bobby getting too close to the truth."

The death of the popular councilman was construed as an accident by news accounts. But to Elmer and Covington's activist supporters, it was no accident.

"They're doin' the same thing to me, and nobody gives a damn except a few of us who speak out," Elmer said.

Cottrell remained focused on the enrollment issue. "I'll check with the tribal authorities about your daughters' tribal enrollment. I'm sure we can get this done," he said.

Elmer asked if he could use Cottrell's copy machine. He needed to make copies of his grandfather's deed and documents he had uncovered about operations at the Mount Tolman project.

"Use whatever you need," Cottrell said.

"I'm looking into the Mount Tolman mining. I need to put together proof that a mother lode of gold was found while taking out that hardening ore. What is it called?"

"Molybdenum—is that what you mean?"

"Yeah, that's it. This is why all that hush money has been paid. Those on the take are protecting the mining company. They're shipping the gold in sixty-gallon barrels to the US government to protect the dollar. It's going east out of Wilbur." Elmer was referring to a small farming community twenty-three miles east of the Grand Coulee Dam.

"Colvilles have been screwed again over rights to our land, this time by AMEX," Elmer persisted. "You know damn well this secret mining of rich deposits of gold could not go on without a wink and a nod from the council and money under the table. I've got proof the gold ore was hidden in the ore shipments that were shipped east.

"Those sons-of-bitches would not mine that cheap ore at a loss. It was the gold-mining operation that kept the mine open. They were taking a hit to cover for the rich gold find. Like I said, barrels were used to hide the gold ore."

"Have you any evidence that barrels were loaded in this manner?"

"I did some snooping around Wilbur and could see where the ore was loaded." As a former game warden and security guard at the Grand Coulee Dam, Elmer knew something about stakeouts. "I checked with locals at the ore sites, and they showed me a bill of lading that indicated unnamed ore samples were forwarded by rail to eastern destinations."

Cottrell asked whether any of the documents indicated that samples had been tested for gold. Elmer said, "No, it's an obvious cover-up. Look at what's going on with the local timber milling company. I've got documents that prove timber had been harvested from property stolen when they built that damn lake." Elmer was convinced Kohler and other councilmen were getting hush money to cover up illegitimate claims going back to the 1930s. Reservation land had been condemned to hold back water of the Columbia River upon completion of the Grand Coulee Dam.

Cottrell remained silent as to the charges of fraudulent claims and possible corruption. There was no direct proof of the allegations. This did not mean he was entirely skeptical of Elmer's charges. Rather, there was not much he could do other than remain in contact with Elmer and focus on his daughters' enrollment.

Many of Elmer's complaints had been voiced at meetings of the grassroots organization formally known as Advocates for Colville Tribes. The movement spawned during the 1970s when the federal government terminated an appeals program to handle disputed deed claims. Known as the Agency Claims Program, advisors were hired on the reservation to help claimants put their appeal in proper order to submit to the Bureau of Indian Affairs (BIA) and, if considered worthy of review, passed on to the federal district attorney.

Tensions grew when the federal government shut down the claims program in December 1979, with no explanation to tribal enrollees. Some claims were still pending, and claimants on appeal felt cheated because there was no obvious way to resolve their disputed claim save for hiring expensive attorneys. Sentiment grew at meetings that the federal government was stonewalling claims petitions.

Sony George, who had worked as advisor to the claims program, filed for a position on the Colville Business Council. Even though in meetings Sony was quite outspoken about corruption, he ran a low-key race, and lost by a large margin. For Elmer and other frustrated claimants, George's loss for the council position meant their claims would be ignored or forgotten.

Elmer intensified his arguments at regional meetings of the grassroots organization. Colvilles needed to take a stand and defend their rights. He insisted that the Indian Bill of Rights passed during the 1960s be honored. Elmer made reference to sections dealing with sovereignty of tribes. He argued it was a fundamental civil right that tribes provide for their own governance over matters such as land disputes.

During this time period, Elmer made regular visits to confront Councilman Kohler over these issues and other matters that dealt with council mismanagement, particularly tribal police conduct. Kohler, an attorney and chair of the tribal business council, listened to Elmer's complaints respectfully, but took no apparent action to resolve his disputes over enrollment or claims to his father's allotment deed.

Over time, Kohler grew increasingly weary of the complaints, and ultimately turned a deaf ear. Elmer bristled at these rebuffs. He saw it as a clear indication that council members were shielding themselves from what they feared the most: how much he knew about council corruption. He repeatedly told those close to him that tribal police had been hired to make a hit on him and his boy. He made it no secret to others that he was armed; he frequently carried a .38 revolver and a hidden .22 Derringer. He would not be defenseless.

The conflict escalated. Elmer confronted the chief of the tribal police, Harry Smiskin, in early April 1986 in a very irate manner. "I know goddamned well the council has a contract on me and my son, and the tribal police are paid to take us out. I just want you to know I'm prepared to defend myself and my family."

Smiskin told Elmer, "You are crazy as hell if you really believe this."

"Just know I'm ready for anything. That's all I'm sayin' at this point," Elmer said.

Smiskin reacted immediately to Elmer's implied threat. He reported his take to Tribal Prosecutor Bob Widdifield, that Elmer McGinnis was armed and prepared to do violence to any officer who might confront him. "Elmer McGinnis is a dangerous man," Smiskin told the prosecutor.

A few days later, Widdifield, Smiskin, and Kohler gathered to decide on the best way to handle what Smiskin argued was an escalating issue. One way or another, Smiskin argued, McGinnis was a threat if something wasn't done in the near term.

Kohler said, "I think we should determine if Elmer has undergone some mental changes."

The threesome resolved that the best way to handle the situation in the near term was to refer Elmer to a mental health professional, Josephine Marcelley, for a mental assessment. Marcelley agreed to do the assessment on the condition that police officers or council members come forward and make a statement if they or others they knew had been personally threatened by McGinnis. Marcelley contacted each council member and the police chief. No one was willing to make a statement. Marcelley called Kohler and said, "I cannot do an assessment absent any claims of threats."

Kohler thought there were others outside the council who would testify as to Elmer's threats. He pressed Marcelley to reconsider doing another mental assessment. "I will agree if you find someone who will make a statement and set up a secure facility to do the assessment," Marcelley said.

Kohler notified the police chief and the prosecutor of the offer. Widdifield suggested the tribal jail could be used for the assessment.

"Then we all agree, right?" Kohler said.

"I'm not sure that's gonna work," Smiskin said. "I don't like the idea of sending my officers to the McGinnis house to pick him up. I know he's got a stash of guns, and those dogs will attack anyone who comes near his place. Maybe we can apprehend him somewhere on the road outside of his home during daylight. I will call Elmer McGinnis and tell him that the police found a stolen gun." He thought a moment longer. "Then I'll tell him that he should drop by the station to help us identify who may have been the original owner." Elmer was an avid gun collector and had bartered guns with locals.

Elmer's mental health assessment was scheduled for April 19, 1986. The plan was initiated. Smiskin made the call about 11:00 a.m. The police chief asked Elmer if he would come down to the office and identify the gun.

Police waited on side streets near Elmer's house for a couple of hours, but he did not emerge.

Around 1:00 p.m., Chief Smiskin got a call from Elmer. He told Smiskin that he would not be coming down to check the weapon. "I've got a wedding to attend in Spokane," he said.

Apparently, someone had leaked to Elmer the plans to have him undergo a mental assessment. The attempted ruse made it clear to Elmer: the council and police would do anything to either put him away or take him out.

Chapter 2

Fair and Square Deal

Ernest B. Brooks, like Elmer McGinnis, was fed up with the federal government's response to disputed claims for land acquisitions and trusts—some going back decades. Brooks, a friend of Elmer, had been terminated in December 1979 as an advisor to the Colville Agency Claims Program, a federally funded program.

The Advocates for Colville Tribes asked Brooks to attend a meeting to explain the purpose of the agency. "We tried to get as many deed claims to Portland as possible before the deadline. The BIA in Portland examined those we sent to them to see that their claims met guidelines," he said. "When I was a claims advisor, we vetted all claims to determine which were possibly legitimate. We forwarded only those claims that likely would be pursued in Spokane. Claims that met BIA guidelines were forwarded to a federal prosecutor for evaluation. If the Spokane district attorney approved the claim, the disputed deed was filed in federal court to adjudicate the claim. We handled over four hundred claims while I was there."

One of the attendees asked, "What makes a legitimate claim?"

"I investigated situations where an allottee was ordered to sign over land to qualify for public assistance, or where someone would want to sell reservation land and apply for a patent fee. I would then determine if the seller actually applied for a patent fee."

Another asked, "What is a land patent?"

"A land patent is evidence of right to the title of a particular tract," Brooks replied. "Basically, I investigated whether such transactions were properly documented."

Another asked if Brooks thought Colville claims would ever be processed.

"Three years after termination of the claims program, I have grown more skeptical of whether any justice will be done for the claims."

Another in the small community conference room in Nespelem asked, "Have you found any shady deals?"

"Yes, I found evidence of suspicious land transactions. And even more frustrating, I read in the Federal Register that a number of them were so low in monetary value for the BIA to file that individuals would have to file these claims on their own if they wanted compensation. I was mainly concerned that, the way things were going, we were going to lose a lot of land and tribal resources.

"Efforts to help those making claims have not gone well since I was released. The costs have been too much for me to get much done. Copying costs at courthouses are fairly high, plus the gas and all. All of us in the claims program fear enrollees may be in danger of losing their Colville land base."

Elmer said, "Give the feds and whites credit—they stole the land fair and square."

The heart of Elmer's discontent, echoed by a minority of local activists, involved long-standing disputes over land and resources. For Colvilles, these disputes could be traced to three major land grabs: the 1863 Lapwai treaty, the federal establishment of the Colville Confederated Tribes Reservation in 1872, and the 1887 Dawes Severalty Act.

Much of the conflict over Northwest territories could be traced back to terms of the Lapwai treaty, where vast expanses of Nez Perce lands were surrendered in exchange for federal protection of any further white incursions. The agreement set the stage for later federal expansions in the Northwest. Chief Lawyer, representing the Nez Perce tribe, signed off on the treaty, believing it would slow white incursion. He sought to preserve Nez Perce village locations and make peaceful agreements, as opposed to taking on an adversary who greatly outnumbered them. Terms of the treaty called for Nez Perces to retreat from over six million acres of Nez Perce territory in Washington and Oregon to locate in Idaho near what is now Lewiston.

Another Nez Perce, Chief Joseph, who resided in the Wallowa region of Oregon, refused to sign the 1863 treaty. Joseph and his Wallowa band resisted terms of the treaty by remaining in their native Wallowa area. They continued to hunt, gather, and construct shelters in the disputed region. Other bands and tribes joined Chief Joseph's band, including White Bird and his band and the Palouse tribe.

In May 1877, Chief Joseph and the rebellious bands and tribes were forced out of the Wallowa area by federal troops led by General Otis Howard. Chief Joseph and White Bird, accompanied by their bands, moved to the north, settling in the Idaho Territory in what is now known as Lewiston and the Camas Prairie.

Three years earlier, Eagle Robe, who was in White Bird's band, had built a shelter on the prairie. A nearby white squatter took exception to the shelter's location and built fences, limiting Eagle Robe's access to his animals and structures. A dispute ensued, and the squatter attacked Eagle Robe, or so claimed Wahlitits, son of Eagle Robe. Eagle Robe was killed.

Vengeance was meted out June 1877. Wahlitits and two members of Chief White Bird's band took revenge on settlers near the Salmon River. The trio believed John Chamberlain had been hostile to Indians. Neighbors reported Chamberlain was viciously attacked and left for dead. Chamberlain's three-year-old daughter was slain, a gaping wound in her neck. Her mother was raped repeatedly. Somehow, she struggled a mile or so to seek help from a neighbor. An arrow had pierced her breast. Witnessing the slaying of her husband and child left her in a severe state of shock. Settlers took her into their home and gave comfort. Swan Lake, a member of the trio who had made the raid, claimed four white men were wounded. No mention was made of women or children.

As the news of the attack spread, whites demanded that something be done. General Howard sent 130 troops to punish the non-treaty tribes and bands and force them to retreat to the boundaries of the Lapwai treaty.

The incident produced a conundrum for Chief Joseph. If his non-treaty bands and tribes fled, it would confirm all were guilty of the violent revenge on settlers. If his Wallowa band and other resisters remained, they would be easily defeated by General Howard's reserve of five thousand troops stationed west of their encampments. It all came down to General Howard's response. Would General Howard engage in a full-scale war on non-treaty tribes and bands?

General Howard had no choice as he saw it. The War of 1877 commenced.

For Chief Joseph's Wallowa band of rebellious natives, the war evolved into clever maneuvering and counterattacks. Some eight hundred non-treaty Indians brilliantly avoided capture along a twelve-hundred-mile journey from Idaho to Bear Paw, near the Canadian border. Engagements ended October 5, 1877. General Miles made a surprise attack on the fourth day of their encampment at Bear Paw, and Chief Joseph was forced to surrender.

While the American press regarded Chief Joseph as a masterful tactician and later tagged him the "Red Napoleon," there was a different view. Yellow Wolf, who fought bravely in the war and was a loyal follower to Chief Joseph, saw his leader differently. He regarded the chief as a peacemaker and a diplomat more than a warrior.

The final bloody battle at Bear Paw resulted in the capture of four hundred Nez Perces. With white flag in hand, Chief Joseph approached General Miles to seek relief for the most vulnerable at Bear Paw—the wounded, the aged, and children. His people were starving and lacking adequate shelter and warmth. The weather had turned cold.

General Miles sent word to Washington, DC that he had captured Chief Joseph and his bands and tribes. Upon surrender, the general promised to return captured Nez Perces and bands to their homeland. The promise was never honored.

Before surrender, over 200 of the non-treaty warriors managed to escape to Canada. Chief White Bird and Yellow Wolf joined Sitting Bull and his Sioux warriors. Yellow Wolf agreed with the other warriors that there could be no peace with whites.

Joseph's Wallowa band was shuttled to various encampments in Kansas and Oklahoma; ultimately, they made a long journey to the Northwest village of Nespelem on the newly-formed Colville Reservation. During the months of transition, the exiled captives suffered from tuberculosis and hunger. Social habits changed. Drinking increased and took its toll. More died from these afflictions than in war. Only 115 exiles survived the trip to the Northwest.

Over the years, Chief Joseph appealed to President Rutherford B. Hayes, Generals Miles and Howard, members of Congress, and academic sympathizers to right the wrongs for his people and other natives. Joseph ceaselessly argued that treaties had been broken to acquire most Nez Perce territories. He pressed gatekeepers in government, the military, and the public at large to join him in petitioning the federal government to honor treaties, return Nez Perce lands, and acknowledge traditional lifestyles.

Chief Joseph witnessed yet other land grabs while exiled on the Colville Reservation. Five years before the 1877 war, the reservation was created to deal with white incursion in the northwest corner of the Washington Territory. On April 9, 1872, President Ulysses S. Grant created the Colville Reservation by executive order to protect tribes and bands from the encroachment of miners and settlers staking claims in the region.

Complaints mounted quickly that too much territory had been ceded to the Indians in forming the reservation. President Grant and his advisors originally set the 1872 boundaries of the Colville Reservation between the Okanogan River to the west and the Idaho Territory boundary to the east. The Columbia River served as the southern boundary, while the 49th parallel represented the northern boundary.

Three months after establishing these boundaries, Congress and the president revised the eastern boundary to be set at the Columbia River. The new boundary was redrawn such that lands west of Kettle Falls and the Columbia River were no longer a part of the reservation, reducing the reservation by one-half.

Twenty years later, settlers and miners making claims on the northern section of the Colville Reservation demanded the boundaries be revised again. Congress yielded to such pressures and moved the northern boundary south, reducing the reservation yet again by roughly one-half. In short, the Colville Reservation was reduced to 2.8 million acres—approximately one-fourth of the original reservation.

Colville lands and resources were diminished even further by the Dawes Severalty Act of 1887, which assimilated native peoples into white culture by giving them an allotment of acreage with the condition they become US citizens.

Over time, Colville enrollees in receipt of the allotments yielded to economic pressures. Hard times forced natives to sell their allotments to supplement their diets and construction of shelters. During the 1920s, newspapers ran ads locally and nationwide of Indian allotments for sale. Adventurers, miners, settlers, and entrepreneurs rushed to make offers.

The volume of sales grew. Critics raised concerns that Indian lands were being lost at such a rate that there would be little reservation land left. In 1934, Congress rescinded the Dawes Act. After the repeal, outsiders continued to seek land, mineral, and timber access on the reservation. Construction of the Grand Coulee Dam resulted in the condemnation of thousands of acres needed to build the large reservoir, Roosevelt Lake. Salmon fishing on the Columbia River, a centuries-old tradition, was virtually eliminated upon completion of the lake.

Elmer McGinnis saw first-hand, during the late 1920s and 1930s, how reservation land was acquired by outsiders. He believed land originally deeded to his grandfather was fraudulently acquired during the sale of allotted parcels of land. Such history weighed on Elmer later in his life. He had served his country and upheld the law as a game warden. After his retirement, it was time to apply the law to exploiters of lands and minerals and put a stop to the corruption.

Chapter 3

Escalation

During the 1986 summer, Lila McGinnis, Elmer's daughter, enjoyed traveling around the reservation on her motorcycle, but needed a car to drive to work and transport her infant. She put her motorcycle up for sale. Don Ferguson, her nearby neighbor from Keller, made an offer, and it was accepted. The bike was delivered to the Fergusons, and Lila McGinnis agreed to put their payment on hold. As weeks went by, Elmer grew impatient. Lila needed the money to apply to her purchase of a Chevrolet Impala.

"I will settle this," Elmer told Lila. Even though his son James had courted and married the Fergusons' daughter, Elmer would not let familial ties get in the way. Elmer drove his pickup east from Nespelem over the Cache Creek Road Pass to the Ferguson residence. The Fergusons had purchased their small home on the outskirts of Keller during the 1940s. Don Ferguson had worked as an electrician on construction of the Grand Coulee and Chief Joseph Dams.

Elmer knocked on the door. Betty Ferguson answered.

"I need to talk with your husband," Elmer said.

"My husband's not home. You need to come back later."

"I and my daughter have waited long enough," Elmer said. "It's time to pay up."

"I don't have the money. You'll have to deal with my husband, Donnie."

"One way or another we are going to get this settled. When is Don coming back?"

"I can't be sure. You need to come back some other time if you want to talk with Donnie."

Elmer erupted, "There will be one less Colville if he doesn't pay up."

"You need to leave right now and come back when Donnie is here," Betty said.

Elmer refused to go. "I will wait for Don, and we'll settle this when he gets back."

Betty Ferguson shut the door. Elmer retreated to his pickup. After a long wait, Elmer left.

Don Ferguson returned much later. His wife repeated Elmer's threat.

"I've got to confront Elmer and let him know he'll get his money, but not with a gun to my head," Ferguson said.

"You will not do any such thing. Elmer's armed, and he was really angry," his wife said.

Don Ferguson yielded to Betty's plea, yet he remained fearful. He decided to make a call to Tribal Prosecutor Bob Widdifield.

"Isn't there something that can be done to protect us? Otherwise, I'll have to move my family out of the area," Ferguson pled. "There's no question Elmer will carry out the threat the next time he shows up."

Widdifield agreed something had to be done. He contacted tribal councilmen about the threat to the Fergusons, and they agreed with the prosecutor. Elmer McGinnis was a dangerous man. Elmer had to be stopped. What could be done?

Councilmen considered their options. Their attempts to have Elmer undergo a mental assessment had proved futile. Maybe another attempt should be made. Widdifield reviewed possible legal remedies. After discussions with council members, he filed a misdemeanor charge in tribal court that Elmer McGinnis had violated the lands trespass statute. By the prosecutor's reasoning, Elmer had illegally entered and remained on the Ferguson homestead when Mrs. Ferguson asked him to leave and he refused.

Widdifield filed a petition for Elmer McGinnis to appear in tribal court on a charge of lands trespass. On August 14, 1986, Anita Dupris, Chief Judge of the Colville tribes, granted the petition and issued a summons.

Chief Smiskin was notified of the judge's decision. Typically, notifications of defendants to appear in court were handled by police and delivered to the defendant's residence.

"That's a very bad idea. I'm not sending any of my officers out to the McGinnis house," Smiskin told Widdifield. "You're looking at a bloodbath if Elmer sees tribal police on his property."

Widdifield agreed. "Maybe we can avoid a showdown. Let's send the warrant by certified mail."

The summons was sent. Elmer was to appear in tribal court on August 29, 1986, at 9:30 a.m.

Elmer picked up his mail on August 18. His anger swelled as he read the notification. "This is a phony, trumped-up charge," he told his daughter Lila. He pointed at the document. "They're plotting to set me up for a hit job." Elmer grabbed a pen and wrote across the envelope in big letters, "Refused."

Upon receiving the unopened summons, Widdifield determined Elmer had to be brought to justice. He filed another petition requesting that the tribal court issue a bench warrant for his arrest, and Judge Dupris signed the warrant. The tribal court handled misdemeanor offenses such as traffic violations and, in this case, the lands trespass charge.

In the meantime, Dale Kohler had not abandoned attempts to have Elmer mentally assessed. He called Marcelley again, and she reiterated her conditions. For any mental assessment, she would need statements from those threatened and a secure facility to conduct the assessment.

Over the next few days, Elmer monitored police activity very closely when driving his pickup for errands. On August 25, 1986, Elmer heard the tribal police dispatcher on his home radio scanner call for police and first responders to cover an accident near Nespelem. Elmer stayed near his scanner, counting the minutes until first responders and police arrived.

Twenty minutes or so later, police and first responders reported they had arrived at the scene. For Elmer, this was totally unacceptable. Police had taken far too much time. Elmer jumped in his pickup and drove to the tribal business council agency to register his complaint. The council office was only blocks away.

Elmer entered the well-maintained council building and forcefully walked into Dale Kohler's office, not waiting for any invitation.

"Why in the hell did it take twenty minutes or more for the police and emergency staff to get to the scene of an accident?" Elmer said. "That's too damn slow to save this young gal if she's in critical condition." His trembling voice grew louder and louder as he lambasted police and emergency responders for not doing their job.

"First responders had reasonably reacted," Kohler said.

Their argument grew in volume as Kohler cited standards for response time, and Elmer insisted they were negligent.

Officers Marconi and Whitney heard the commotion and entered Kohler's office. Both heard Kohler repeat that tribal officers had responded appropriately, yet Elmer's growing anger was apparent. The officers tried to calm Elmer, stating they were only there to prevent anything from getting out of hand. "If you calm down," Whitney said, "we'll leave the office and let you discuss this with Councilman Kohler."

Elmer grew more agitated and shouted, "Get the hell out of my face. You rookies don't know the first thing about the law or why you're even here."

"You're out of line," Whitney said.

Elmer grew angrier. "There's the door. Now leave, you assholes, so I can settle this with Dale."

"Elmer, could you lower your voice and sit down? If so, we'll leave the office," Whitney said.

"Stick it up your ass."

"You are under arrest," Whitney said.

"For what?" Elmer demanded. "Show me a warrant."

"The chief has the papers," Whitney said.

Moments later, Chief Smiskin appeared at Kohler's door. He looked directly at Elmer. "Here's a copy of an arrest warrant for you on a lands trespass charge." Smiskin handed Elmer the warrant.

Elmer briefly looked at it, wadded it up, and threw it on the floor. He screamed, "You do not have a proper warrant to make any arrest. Take it and shove it up your ass."

Chief Smiskin rushed forward and shoved Elmer against a file cabinet. Officers Whitney and Marconi grabbed Elmer's arms to keep him from falling. Elmer resisted by kicking and pulling his arms from their grip. The three officers shoved Elmer to the floor and forcibly restrained him. In the struggle, they turned Elmer face down and brought his hands to his back. Elmer fought even harder when they attempted to cuff him.

"Get your hands off me, you sons of bitches!" Elmer screamed. "It's my heart, you idiots. I've got pain in my chest."

Smiskin shouted to Kohler, "Get an ambulance."

Elmer continued to struggle with the police on the floor. He threw his arms and kicked an officer. After several futile attempts to restrain him, Marconi grabbed Elmer's chest from behind, and Whitney grabbed one leg while Smiskin grabbed the other. Elmer was lifted and taken out of the office toward the front lawn of the agency.

Elmer screamed, "Get your hands off me! I need to take my pills."

Wendell George, a business council member, and John Smith with the Fish and Wildlife Department were outside Kohler's office, ran out to Elmer's pickup, and located two pill bottles. They rushed back and offered the pills to Elmer.

Elmer grew even angrier and yelled, "Get that goddamn thing out of here. Who got in my pickup? You had no authority to get into my pickup."

Kohler made a call for first responders. EMTs William Joseph and Kelly

Manley arrived in minutes from the nearby fire station to take vital signs and listen to his heart. Elmer, seeing the EMTs, threw his arms and legs in every direction to free himself from the officers' restraint.

EMTs joined the fracas, attempting to put Elmer on a gurney, but it was futile. Officers Whitney and Marconi grabbed him under each arm. EMTs held his feet, and he was forced down on the lawn. Elmer fought even harder as the foursome rolled him over on his stomach and forced his arms behind him. He was handcuffed.

"Are you going calm down so we can get you to Indian Health Services?" Marconi asked. Elmer said nothing. As he was brought to his feet, he no longer resisted. Two officers held each arm, walked him toward a police car, and placed him in the back seat.

Arriving at the emergency entrance to the spartan structure near the edge of town, Elmer exited the car without incident. Dr. Patricia Ann Weber was on duty in the emergency room.

Elmer still had not calmed down. While waiting in the examining room for the doctor, Elmer yelled, "You sons of bitches have broken the law. You have no authority to arrest me." The police remained silent.

Dr. Weber appeared. Elmer said, "Get these goons out of here."

"I can handle the patient at this point," the doctor said. The police uncuffed Elmer and left.

Elmer fumbled in his pants pocket and pulled out a gun. He gave it to Dr. Weber. The .22-caliber Derringer was something of a surprise, given that tribal police should have searched for weapons.

"Will you hide it for me?" Elmer asked.

To humor him, Dr. Weber placed the gun on a tray under paper towels.

The physical exam produced no conclusive evidence of a heart attack. She wrote in her notes that further observation was needed. Dr. Weber gave him a nitroglycerin pill for his heart and Valium to calm him down. She requested to transfer Elmer to the Grand Coulee Dam Hospital for follow-up tests on his heart.

Police transported Elmer to the hospital, twenty miles south of Nespelem. The medication had calmed him, and the trip was without incident. Dr. William Sheldon conducted cardiac tests on Elmer and found no evidence of a heart attack. Elmer gave his account of what had happened.

"They'll kill me if they get another shot at it," Elmer said.

Dr. Sheldon listened without comment. After leaving the examining room, he talked with the officers. It was evident to him that Elmer needed a psychiatric examination.

Dr. Sheldon called Josephine Marcelley and left a message to call back soon so arrangements could be set up for a mental assessment. After a long wait, he called again. Marcelley answered and asked who was being referred.

"I would like you to assess a recent patient who believes police have been contracted to kill him," the doctor replied. "His name is Elmer McGinnis."

"I will only conduct an assessment in a secure facility, not the hospital ER," Marcelley insisted. "As an alternative, I will do one if it is conducted in the tribal jail." Marcelley called Smiskin and asked if the patient could be assessed in the tribal jail.

Smiskin refused. "A more secure holding facility would be required." He called Okanogan County Jail officials to determine if a transfer could be made from the Coulee Dam Hospital to their holding facility. Jail authorities agreed, and arrangements were made for transportation.

Smiskin made another call to Marcelley. "Elmer is being transferred to the Okanogan County Jail. This is a secure facility you asked for. When can you do a mental health assessment?"

"I appreciate your efforts to find a secure area, but the county jail is out of my catchment area," Marcelley said.

Tribal police handcuffed Elmer and placed him in a police car. The sixty-mile drive from the ER facility to Okanogan was tranquil. Elmer was tired and in pain. On arrival, Elmer was processed and assigned to a cell.

After Elmer had settled, the on-duty jail officer checked on him. He observed that Elmer seemed to be in great pain. His breathing was labored, and he was doubled over. The officer thought Elmer was having a heart attack. Walter Carnicel, a physician's assistant, was called to assess his condition. Carnicel completed his examination and agreed with the jailer that Elmer may have had a coronary attack. An ambulance was summoned. Elmer was rushed to Mid-Valley Hospital emergency room in Omak, some ten minutes to the north.

The jail administrator, Larry Thomas, contacted tribal police and notified them that Elmer McGinnis was no longer in their custody. Tribal police were responsible for Elmer while he was a patient at the Mid-Valley Hospital.

Smiskin directed Tribal Sergeant Gary Carden to meet Thomas at the ER to oversee the transfer from the jail to the hospital. Officer Carden arrived shortly after Thomas. He entered the ER and was directed to the examining room. Carden refused to go inside. Instead, he peered through a glass partition out of Elmer's view, watching staff examine him. Thomas remained with Elmer as staff completed their exam.

After status reports from staff, Thomas exited the examining room. He spotted Sergeant Carden and gave him an update.

The two considered custody arrangements. "It's best I stay out of view—no need to upset him," Carden said.

"The heart monitor attached to Elmer McGinnis has an alarm," Thomas said. "He's not going far without staff knowing it."

"I've got to get back to the jail. He is going to be your prisoner," Thomas said.

"I'll call my chief and update him as to Elmer's status," Carden said.

Sergeant Carden called Smiskin to discuss custody arrangements. Carden assured Smiskin that Elmer was not going anywhere given his medical condition. If he were to exit, the alarm hooked to his heart monitor would alert staff. Smiskin agreed with Carden that Elmer was not at risk to escape. A few hours later, Sergeant Carden left the ER facility.

As to Elmer's physical condition, staff medical reports were conflicting.

Fractured ribs and a possible coronary attack had been noted in Elmer's chart. Some nursing staff observed bruises, while others failed to note any signs of bodily trauma. A radiologist examined X-rays and could not confirm the presence of rib fractures.

Chapter 4

Escape or Discharge?

Lila McGinnis was notified by her Aunt Francis Orr that her dad had been arrested and was in the Mid-Valley Hospital. Lila rushed to the phone and relayed the news to her elder sister, Francis Peoples. Lila also contacted her younger sisters, Elsie and Laura, and brothers, James McGinnis and Patrick Hoffman. Lila agreed to drive her Chevrolet Impala to pick up Elsie, Francis, and Patrick, who lived in Keller.

Lila made a call to Bob Widdifield in Nespelem, who invited the family to his office. Francis asked, "What happened to Dad? Why is he in the hospital?"

"Your dad got in a scuffle with police when they tried to arrest him," Widdifield said. "He got in an argument with Dale Kohler over police response to an accident. When police tried to arrest him for lands trespass, he became very combative."

"Is this over Don Ferguson not paying for my motorcycle?" Lila asked.

"That's only part of the story. Elmer made a threat to Don Ferguson and refused to leave their place," Widdifield said.

"How does that explain Dad being sent to a hospital?" Francis said.

"He had a heart attack in jail. That's why he ended up at Mid-Valley," Widdifield said.

"We hear he got beat up?" Francis said.

"Your dad resisted arrest. He had heart pains while officers attempted to restrain him," Widdifield said. "If there were any injuries, I'm unaware of them."

"We want to see Dad," Francis said. "Is that possible?"

"I don't see any problem with that. Maybe that will calm him," Widdifield said.

Late afternoon on August 26, the McGinnis daughters, along with Patrick, quickly gathered items, such as Elmer's favorite chewing tobacco and a razor, from his home in Nespelem and made their way to Omak to check on their father. Patrick drove them to a parking spot just outside the entrance to Mid-Valley Hospital, and they were directed to Elmer's room, not far from a nurse's station.

Nurse Diane Peterson was on her swing shift. She stepped in to check on her patient, Elmer McGinnis. Elmer was resting peacefully with an oxygen tube in his nose and was hooked to an IV. His eyes were closed. As the nurse came near his bed, Elmer roused from his sleep.

Elmer had been transferred from the ER to the ward the previous day. His heart monitor was still in place. No tribal police were present. The nurse reviewed Elmer's chart. "How are you feeling?"

"My ribs are really sore. Could you bring me more water?"

"Sure."

Elmer's daughters, Lila, Elsie, and Francis, appeared at Elmer's door.

"Hi, Dad. How are you doing?" Lila asked.

"I'm just resting, trying to recover from the beating," Elmer answered. "They nearly killed me."

Elmer paused to get a breath. "Smiskin put a knee to my back and pulled my throat back—nearly suffocated me. Another cop twisted my arm behind me while the other one punched me with a gut shot."

His daughter Lila sobbed when hearing this. "Dad, how could they do this to you?"

"I've been telling you all along they're out to kill me. They nearly got it done. Look at where they cut my finger when they knocked me to the ground to cuff me," Elmer said while showing his wound.

Elmer turned to Nurse Peterson. "Where's my meds? I need to take my phenobarbital."

"The doctor prescribed the drug for twice a day. Your next dosage is scheduled for this evening around 8:00 p.m.," the nurse said.

"Damnit, my prescription calls for three times a day, not two," Elmer said.

To mollify Elmer, Nurse Peterson yielded and gave him his medication. A few hours early might not make that much difference. Lila asked Nurse Peterson about the possibility of Elmer's release.

"I'll check with Dr. Justus. Your dad needs time to recover from injuries and a possible heart attack," Nurse Peterson said.

After leaving Elmer's room, the ward nurse took her break to meet with Dr. Justus, Elmer's attending physician.

"He needs medical attention for a few more days," Dr. Justus said over a cup of coffee in the cafeteria, "but his health insurance won't cover the costs."

"So what do you recommend?" Nurse Peterson asked.

"I'm willing to discharge him on the condition his family is willing to provide follow-up care at his home, making sure he takes his meds and gets plenty of rest."

Later, Dr. Justus stopped by Elmer's room. Family members were gathered around Elmer.

"How are you feeling, Elmer?" asked the doctor.

"I still have a lot of pain from the beating, but I need to get back to the house to care for the animals and take care of Laura."

"I think you would benefit to stay a couple more days," the doctor said.

"Maybe so, but my daughter Laura needs someone to be at the place. She's got homework and chores," Elmer said.

"Okay, but on the condition that your family provides care for you until you get back on your feet," said the doctor. "You've got some heart issues, and you need your rest."

Dr. Justus left to write up the discharge papers, and Nurse Peterson exited to attend to another patient.

"I've got to get the hell outta here," Elmer said. Family members agreed. "We can't let them get another shot at killing me."

"We'll get you out. The doctor just said he would discharge you," Lila said. Patrick helped his dad get dressed.

Nurse Peterson finished her rounds and returned to the nursing station to fill out notes for Elmer's discharge. While she completed the paperwork, her supervisor informed her there was a police hold on the patient. Nurse Peterson quickly located the ward clerk. "Call the tribal police and sheriff's office to clarify Elmer McGinnis's legal status," she said.

The ward clerk called the tribal police dispatcher, who said they had no information about the patient Elmer McGinnis. The clerk then made a call to the Okanogan County Sheriff's Department and asked if they had a hold on Elmer.

"We have no hold order on Elmer McGinnis—the patient was in the custody of the Colville Tribal Police," the officer said.

The clerk thought something was amiss. She made another call to the Colville Tribal Police and asked if Elmer had been released. After further review, the dispatcher said that there was a hold on Elmer McGinnis.

Nurse Peterson realized Elmer's discharge was in question. The nurse approached his room and saw that Elmer was dressed. "Mr. McGinnis, you need to wait for your discharge papers and get your medications from the pharmacy," she said. Elmer remained mute as Francis steadied him on his feet. The nurse left Elmer's room to put together his forms and his meds. Minutes later, Nurse Peterson returned to his room. Elmer and the family had left.

She spotted Elmer with his family in the hallway. The nurse caught up with the patient. "Mr. McGinnis, please wait until I find you a wheelchair."

Elmer continued to move toward the hospital exit.

"Sir, you need to wait. Apparently the police need to talk with you," Nurse Peterson said. Elmer was undeterred. Nurse Peterson grabbed his arm. "You might as well wait, sir. They need to talk to you. Either wait here, or they'll probably just come after you."

"That's not true. The jailer told us when we picked up Dad's stuff that he was no longer under their custody," Francis said.

Lila added, "Yes, Dad's been cleared of whatever charges have been brought against him."

Elmer McGinnis said nothing. It was clear he was not about to comply. As he approached the front nursing station and exit, Elmer yelled to his girls, "Come on. We're leaving."

Nurse Peterson hurried to her station to locate and update Dr. Justus. The doctor was with another patient. She asked that the doctor step outside for a moment. "Elmer McGinnis is leaving the hospital, and he has a police hold on him. He did not take any of his medications with him," she said.

"Try to stop him if it's not too late. Make sure he has his prescriptions," Dr. Justus said.

Nurse Peterson hurriedly returned to the hospital entrance. She saw a car pull away, maybe a Chevrolet Impala. The car headed north along Okoma Drive.

Nurse Peterson returned to her station frustrated. At a minimum, she decided it best to chart what she had observed. She indicated on chart notes that Dr. Justus had discharged the patient to the care of his family. Further, she noted the ward clerk had notified tribal and county police of the discharge, and "the patient would not wait per RN request for tribal police." Nurse Peterson was a health provider, not a cop. Her focus was to make sure the discharge orders had been followed.

In the car, Elmer made it clear to the family he was not about to remain in the hospital to be turned over to tribal police and risk exposure to another beating. Given no tribal police had been assigned to guard Elmer, Lila felt, as did other family members, that their dad was free to go.

Hospital staff notified tribal police that Elmer was discharged and had left the hospital. Chief Smiskin took quick action, notifying tribal officers that Elmer and his family likely were headed for Disautel Pass, en route to the McGinnis house in Nespelem. It was clear to the tribal police chief: Elmer was a fugitive. He had escaped custody. Elmer was dangerous and had to be stopped.

Chapter 5

Desperate Journey

Chief Smiskin directed Tribal Officer Chester Clark to cover Highway 155, the scenic Disautel Pass. "Likely, Elmer is headed home," the chief said. Clark was in Nespelem at the time. He raced his car up the pass toward Omak. Smiskin advised Clark to look for an Impala.

Near the summit around 8:00 p.m., Clark saw a car traveling in the opposite direction that seemed to fit the description of the car pulling away from the hospital. The officer thought he recognized the driver as Patrick Hoffman. He also identified at least two of the McGinnis daughters. He guessed Elmer was sitting in the back of the car.

Clark made a sharp U-turn and pursued the Impala, accelerating to catch them. He observed the Impala make a sharp turn down a logging road toward Armstrong Meadows. As the dust cloud became thicker, Clark halted his pursuit after a quarter-mile chase and called for a backup officer. It was too risky to go any farther with all the dust. He didn't want to be ambushed.

Tribal Officer Cox was maybe fifteen to thirty minutes away. Cox raced to the turnoff and drove a short distance to the Armstrong Meadows logging road, recognizing his partner ahead. They conferred with each other. Cox agreed with Clark that it was too dangerous to go any farther.

Clark updated dispatch of the danger of pursuing the Impala with all the dust. "The dust is thick, and it is hard to see anything. How should we proceed?"

"Stand by. I'll patch you in to Dick," replied the dispatcher.

Assistant Chief of Tribal Police John Dick, who was doing his own search for the Impala, radioed Clark. "Stay put until I get there."

Patrick accelerated the Impala miles down the logging road toward Armstrong Meadows. He pushed the car to the limit, bouncing over the rock-laden road. Francis kept a lookout for police. Elsie and Laura were in the back seat with their dad. Francis sat next to Patrick in the middle, with Lila on the passenger's side. The dust settled as the road turned to gravel and rocks, and Francis told Patrick, "They are out of sight. I can't see any sign of them."

Elmer yelled, "Stop the car. I want to get out."

Patrick slammed on the brakes. Elmer got out of the car, as did Patrick. It was chilly as dusk approached. Elmer, with little hesitancy, made it clear. "I'm headed home. There's no way I'm going to jail. They'll have to kill me first."

Lila strongly protested. "Dad, you are in no condition to make it back over these hills."

"I don't want you girls to be caught in the line of fire," Elmer said.

"But you are weak and don't have a coat or any water."

"By God, I'm not gonna let them have a second chance to take me out. I've got to get back to the house," Elmer said. "You girls make tracks to get back without me in the car. I need to get back to feed the animals and get my legal matters handled."

Patrick thought over his options. His dad was in bad shape. The cross-country terrain, with steep declines and thickets of brush and trees, would be a challenge for anyone during daylight hours. Patrick had no choice as he saw it. He was not about to let his dad make the hike across mountainous backcountry late at night and solo. Elmer had complained of pain during the trip. Patrick guessed that with his dad's weakened condition, it would be a long shot at best to make it back home before the next day. He guessed it was quite a distance, maybe fifteen miles to get there. "There's no way I'm going to let you go back home on your own," Patrick told his father.

Elmer's daughters pled to their dad again. "You are in no condition to hike anywhere," Francis said.

Lila said, "You have no coat or anything to make it back."

"Don't worry. I'll make sure Dad is safe and cared for," Patrick told his sisters.

Francis offered her coat. The other daughters followed suit to find one that would fit Patrick.

Patrick opened the trunk. Elmer and Patrick inspected the contents. Patrick's gym bag contained firearms, ammunition, and nunchucks, along with some clothing—a bandana, a stocking cap, and a swimming suit. Elmer's personal belongings from the county jail, a flare gun, and flares were also in the mix of items in the trunk. Patrick grabbed his gym bag and added the flare gun and flares.

The two quickly disappeared into the bush. Lila, Francis, Elsie, and Laura shed tears as they made their way back to the car. The sisters all had the same fear—their dad would not make it. "You know Dad. When he makes a decision, there is no turning back," Francis told Lila.

"We have no other option now but to get back to the highway," Lila said.

The first ridge in the mountainous terrain proved to be a challenge. Elmer crawled in a few spots over rocks to make his way down a slope covered with alpine trees and scrub. Elmer did not have the strength to remain upright. There was no trail, only vaguely familiar land sites in the distance. The late-summer setting sun offered little light.

Elmer's strength continued to decline. Patrick did his best to help his dad negotiate some of the rougher terrain. They had traveled only two miles. Patrick piggy-backed his dad at that point, as the two had decided to make their way to the North Star Valley. The heavy gym bag added another challenge for Patrick.

"Maybe if we make it to the valley, we can find water, and let the girls know where we are," Patrick said.

"Let's keep going," Elmer said. Patrick was struggling to maintain any kind of pace. His back and leg muscles burned. Patrick's strength was weakening. He guessed their destination was still miles away.

In the meantime, Lila drove her Impala back to Highway 155 and traveled in the direction of Omak and then back toward Nespelem, attempting to avoid police contact.

"Somehow we have got to contact Dad's attorney and let him know Dad is out there, exposed to the cold and very weak," Lila said.

Her sisters agreed. "Something has to be done if Dad has any chance of surviving the backcountry," Francis said.

"Let's head for Ives's place in the valley, make a call to Bill Cottrell, and see if there's something he can do to get the police to back off," Lila said.

Fifteen-year-old Laura McGinnis knocked on the door and asked Mr. Ives if they could use his phone. Mr. Ives invited the McGinnis daughters in and directed Lila to the phone, who called Bill Cottrell. It was around 10:00 p.m.

With tears flowing, Lila told Cottrell, "They're going to kill my dad. What can be done to stop this?"

"Try to calm yourself. I'll contact the tribal prosecutor and see if we can get the police to back off," the attorney offered. "I'll try to get him to agree to your dad making a court appearance in the morning."

"Dad's in no shape to go to a hearing. You have to stop the police," Lila said.

"The best way to make this happen is to find a way for your dad to agree to an appearance," Cottrell said.

With a tone of desperation and more tears, Lila said, "The police beat him up severely. What will they do next?"

Cottrell tried to calm Lila. "I'll contact the tribal prosecutor and advise him that Elmer and I will show up tomorrow morning. I'll do my best to persuade the prosecutor to call off the search." After a short pause, Cottrell added, "We need to get back to Elmer and tell him about the offer, that we will voluntarily submit to a mental health assessment if police will call off the search."

"Dad may not survive the night," Lila said.

Cottrell agreed. "This is why we need to get this agreement with Widdifield, so we can contact your dad and get him home."

After Lila hung up and departed, Mr. Ives, who overheard Lila's conversation, immediately called Councilman Wendell George.

"I just overheard Lila McGinnis chatting with Bill Cottrell. I think you ought to let Harry Smiskin know what's going on," Ives told George.

George agreed. Elmer McGinnis was dangerous and needed to be apprehended. The councilman notified Chief Smiskin of the phone conversation the McGinnis daughters had with Cottrell.

Chief Smiskin grabbed his gear and returned to his Nespelem office. It was clear to Smiskin that Elmer and his son Patrick were headed for home. Elmer was a major risk if he were to get to his arsenal of weapons.

The police chief asked the dispatcher to contact the officers assigned to the search and report their location.

Assistant Tribal Chief John Dick, who was still on duty, reported that he was in the Star Valley area and saw no sign of Elmer. Officers from the Okanogan Sheriff's Office and the Washington State Patrol responded that they had surveilled Disautel Pass. They had nothing to report.

Smiskin sketched out a rough plan to the dispatcher. "Tell officers to concentrate on roads between Star Valley and Nespelem."

Around 11:00 p.m., Brian Phillips, a rookie, spotted an Impala along Highway 155. He raced to catch the car and turned on his light bar. The car moved to the side. Phillips called for backup. He approached the driver's side of the Impala with light in hand and recognized Lila McGinnis. Lila rolled her window down.

"Get out of the car with your hands clearly visible!" screamed Phillips.

Lila slowly brought her hands up.

"Now get out of the car very carefully. I want to see both your hands," he yelled.

As Lila pushed the door slowly open, Phillips directed his police-issued .38 revolver against Lila's head.

The force of the gun against her temple was painful. Lila's heart raced as she feared any moment the trigger would be pulled.

Phillips grabbed her arm and directed her to his police car. The gun remained firmly pressed against her head. Her heart raced faster as she feared each step might cause a discharge.

Phillips did a pat-down, opened the back door, and shoved Lila into the back seat.

At the same time, Chester Clark, who was only a few miles away, responded to Phillips's backup request. He carefully approached the Impala. Clark came up behind Francis, who was seated in the passenger side of the car. Clark pulled his revolver, opened the door, and put a gun to her head. He directed her to Phillips's police car, patted her down, and placed her in the back seat with Lila. Clark returned to the Impala with gun in hand and directed Elsie and Laura to his car. Both officers returned to their cars and headed for tribal police headquarters in Nespelem.

For Lila and Francis, this confirmed Dad was right. The patriarch of the family had said over and over to his daughters that the police would kill him if they ever got the chance. Their treatment by police convinced them he was right. Their dad would be gunned down if ever found.

About a half hour after the daughters were taken to tribal police headquarters, Widdifield called Bill Cottrell to ask if he had seen Elmer or knew of his whereabouts. The attorney said he had not seen him or had any idea where he might be. The tribal prosecutor then asked if Cottrell had received a phone call from Lila McGinnis.

"I have not received any call or made contact whatsoever with Elmer McGinnis this evening," Cottrell said. "Look, this is a very dangerous situation. It's only a matter of time before police will encounter my client and hostilities will break out. Only one shot need be fired by anybody, and all kinds of bad things could happen. You have the authority to diffuse the situation," he said. "You are the only one who has contact with either side."

"First, your client needs to surrender peacefully," the prosecutor said.

"There is a way to halt any volatile encounter. We would agree to appear at a mental hearing or arraignment or whatever you want to set up in the morning."

Widdifield hung up and contacted Chief Smiskin. "I just talked to Bill Cottrell about Elmer. He lied to me when he said he had not received a phone call. I don't trust him."

"Don't worry. We're still on the lookout for Elmer," Smiskin said.

Police interrogated Lila and Francis about their dad's whereabouts. The two daughters told police they had no idea where their dad might be. Police believed both were holding out. Francis, being the oldest and having status as a Colville enrollee, was placed into custody. Ostensibly, she was charged with aiding and abetting an escape, though later it was unclear whether the charge was ever revealed to her. Lila remained in the back of Phillips's car for two hours without a bathroom break. Later she was transferred to Okanogan County Jail and released.

Elsie and Laura were not charged with any crime. At some point, police decided each would be released. Elsie had not played a role in the exodus from the hospital and was not enrolled as a Colville. Laura's status as a juvenile was considered. After processing, Laura was released from custody to her Aunt Francis Orr.

Around midnight, Elmer and Patrick found their way to the west valley floor near Nespelem. Patrick was exhausted. His muscles acutely burned. It was cold. There was no water. Somehow they had reached a point approximately two or three miles from Nespelem. Patrick had carried Elmer for much of the journey.

"We have to make camp. We need the rest. Let's settle under that grove of trees and wait the night out," Patrick implored.

"Let's get home. We need to keep moving," Elmer said. "It's not that far. We can make it…I know we can."

"I think it best we stop for a while. We're safe here," Patrick said.

Elmer would not hear of it. "There's too much at stake. I gotta get this mess settled." Elmer's ribs were sore. He was weak, and the medication had made him a little drowsy. The pair slowly made their way another mile or so. Patrick again suggested to his stubborn dad that they call it a night and check in with the neighbors living nearby. Elmer persisted. He had to take care of his dogs and get his legal problems resolved.

Around 1:00 a.m., struggling with each step, they reached a hillside overlooking the Cache Creek Road, not far from Elmer's driveway. Patrick and Elmer scanned the road, looking for signs of a police presence. The pair did not see Officer Phillips's police car to the east.

Elmer was exhausted. The duo had done the impossible—home at last.

Chapter 6

Tribal War

Around midnight, Chief Smiskin called his officers back to headquarters to outline a plan for the remainder of the night. The late-night shift was about over. Wendell George's call reporting the Cottrell phone call was viewed as alarming. Given Patrick was not with his sisters, he likely had accompanied Elmer, and they were headed for home. However, officers also felt the risk of Elmer reaching his house to access his weapons cache was unlikely given Elmer's condition and the challenging terrain. Perhaps the search should be called off until morning. A consensus emerged.

Chief Smiskin laid out his plan. Assistant Chief John Dick was told to go on home. Other officers, Sergeant Lou Millard and Sergeant Gary Carden, were given the night off. As a note of caution, Chief Smiskin assigned Officer Brian Phillips to watch duty east of the McGinnis property. Officer Chester Clark was told to continue his search for the pair.

Tribal police remained fearful that if Elmer reached his residence and gained access to his arsenal of weapons, a deadly battle could break out.

Phillips drove to the McGinnis house and parked his police car to the east, out of view. A streetlight illuminated Cache Creek Road to the west near Elmer's driveway.

Around 1:00 a.m., Phillips was roused by someone appearing under the streetlight. He looked again, and then he was certain. There were two men crossing Cache Creek Road. He quickly reached for his mike and made a call to dispatch. "I can't be certain it's Elmer or his son, but I definitely saw two men crossing Cache Creek Road," Phillips reported. "Maybe it was a couple of drunks from the War Bonnet."

The rookie officer was not sure what to do next. Maybe it was best to check in with Millard, someone he looked up to in his early apprenticeship as the cop who could be counted on to make the right call. Millard was on his way home to Keller when he got Phillips's call. "I just spotted two men, maybe drunks crossing Cache Creek Road. What do you recommend?"

"It could be Elmer and his son. They may have reached the house," Millard said. "Try to intercept them."

"It's too dark to see anyone."

"Then drive your car to the east side of the McGinnis place, and park on the small dirt road just off Cache Creek Road. Wait for me to get there."

Sergeant Millard was the officer whom others on the tribal force looked up to in dangerous situations. He had made raids in drug busts where occupants were known to be armed and dangerous. Millard did a U-turn and headed toward the McGinnis home.

After being notified of two men crossing Cache Creek Road, Smiskin directed Chester Clark to head for Elmer's home. He contacted Bill Joseph, an EMT who was off for the night, and directed him to drive a rescue vehicle to Cache Creek Road. Joseph arrived shortly and parked his rig on Cache Creek Road. He turned floodlights onto the McGinnis house and beyond.

Smiskin decided to play it safe. He had been notified by an unknown source of an arrest warrant for Patrick for simple assault in Ferry County. He ordered the dispatcher to notify all available officers to make their way to the McGinnis house.

Not realizing police had spotted them making a dash across Cache Creek Road, Elmer and Patrick hurried down the long drive to the McGinnis house. The exhausted pair was anxious to get inside.

"We made it. Now we can get some water and get off our feet," Elmer said.

The last mile had been brutal. Approaching the west-side entrance, Elmer reached in his pocket for keys. None were found.

Elmer tried to open the door. It was locked. "Damnit. I left the keys in my pickup," Elmer said. "It's parked back at the police station."

"Yeah, Laura got them yesterday," Patrick said.

Officer Clark pulled into the long McGinnis driveway and directed his headlights toward Elmer's van parked near the entrance to the house.

Elmer's and Patrick's muscles tightened as the headlights exposed their silhouettes, or so it seemed. They were partially hidden by the van.

Elmer moved to the south end of the van. "We've got no choice. We've gotta get away from the house," Elmer said with a muffled voice. "Let's make a run for the chicken coop." The lights from Clark's auto made it risky. Even more problematic, Joseph had directed bright search lights from the rescue vehicle toward the backyard. Sections of the chicken coop to the south were exposed, given the building was elevated on a ridge.

Looking for dark areas in the backyard, the two worked their way to the east side of the coop and hunkered behind it. Patrick placed his gym bag near the east corner of the coop, which housed Elmer's fighting chickens. The cage doors were on the north side, opposite from where they hunkered down.

The three lights mounted on the rescue rig were intense despite their distance of roughly 150 yards from the coop.

"Let's stay low. Maybe they'll go away," Patrick whispered to Elmer as the bright lights exposed the northern side of the chicken coop.

"Make sure you stay away from the lights," Elmer said.

Police continued to arrive at the McGinnis house. Chester Clark remained in his car with high beams aimed toward the driveway. Sergeant Millard arrived shortly thereafter, followed by Sergeant Gary Carden. Assistant Chief John Dick was the last to arrive.

Dick had the longest drive to make—around twenty minutes from Elmer City. He had just turned in for the night when he got the call about two men crossing Cache Creek Road. He grabbed his Second Chance vest and gear. Arriving minutes after Millard, Dick gathered officers near Clark's car. Dick, Millard, Carden, and Phillips sketched out how they should proceed. The search would start with abandoned houses in front of the McGinnis house.

Guns were drawn as they searched the first old house to the north. There were no signs of anyone inside or signs of having been occupied. They searched the second house to the south, and also found it empty. They considered their options. "Why don't we take a look at that abandoned pickup east of the McGinnis house," Dick said.

"Let's go," said Millard.

Phillips followed without comment. Sergeant Carden likewise deferred to Dick's directive and tagged behind Millard and Phillips. Then Carden halted and addressed the threesome ahead of him. "Think I'll cover the west side of the house."

Carden made his way to the driveway lit up by Clark's headlights. He approached the van and hunkered down behind it relative to the side entrance of the house. He directed his flashlight to the door and windows on the west side of the house, spotting nothing of note. He remained behind the van, taking extra precaution. He worried that Elmer and Patrick could be in the house, armed and prepared to ambush anyone approaching the door.

Dick, Millard, and Phillips cautiously made their way to the abandoned pickup on the east side of the McGinnis house. They directed their high-powered flashlights at potential hiding spots, starting with the inside of the cab. Their search again showed no signs of the two men. Dick directed Phillips to get word to the EMT. "Tell him to turn off those damn floodlights," Dick ordered. "Backlighting makes us easy targets."

Dick and Millard moved south from the pickup along the east boundary fence of the McGinnis property. "Let's check the woodpile," Dick said. The woodpile was in the backyard, just west of the fence line. Dick shined his light along the fence line, trying to find a place to cross. Millard was not far behind. Phillips remained at the abandoned pickup.

Dick found a low spot midway and waited for Millard. Dick shoved the fence awkwardly down with his boot to allow Millard to make his way over. Dick took his turn. "We need to shed a few pounds," Dick joked as he struggled to clear the fence. Both laughed.

Once they crossed into the McGinnis backyard, the two officers directed their lights downward to avoid a stumble. They headed south. Thumping sounds to the south alerted the duo. Dick and Millard beamed their lights toward the southern fence line of the property.

Two large eyes reflected their light beams. A black or brown horse starred at them and stomped its hoof. "Easy, boy," Dick said quietly. The duo continued southwest toward what looked like a chicken coop.

As the floodlights were doused, Elmer grew tense. Something was up. His alarm heightened as he tracked two beams of light on the ground approaching the coop. "I'll cover this side," he whispered. Patrick opened the gym bag and exposed a holstered .45 semiautomatic, a .22 revolver, and a 9-millimeter assault pistol. Elmer grew tenser. Each grabbed a weapon.

Patrick could not spot anyone on the west side approaching the coop. Lights from the car in the driveway partially exposed anyone moving in their direction. As the two lights approached the coop from the east, Patrick moved toward the middle of the coop. Elmer intensely watched the lead light move toward the coop and partially disappear. The mesmerizing light momentarily was directed to the north side of the chicken coop. Seconds later, it reappeared. The beam flashed from high to low along the east wall of the coop. The beam moved toward Elmer. He crouched even lower.

Elmer's autonomic nervous system was on full alert. His eyes dilated. His heart redlined. Elmer gripped his firearm tighter. The light got closer and closer and closer. The beam of light was directed at his head.

A shot was fired.

As Dick turned to check on Lou, he felt a bullet rip through his chest. Dick caught a glimpse of an orange flash over his left shoulder. The impact knocked him to the ground.

Millard fired two rounds toward the coop.

Dick felt blood as he struggled to get to his feet, but his heavy body was too much.

"I'm hit," Dick yelled in desperation.

"John, if you're hit, get down," Millard yelled back.

Dick was terrified as he heard more shots fired, but he could not tell from what direction. He slowly got his bearings and crawled toward where he thought Lou might be. The sky lit up above him as a flare ignited overhead.

More shots were fired. He still could not see Lou. The flare lit the backyard and exposed him. He felt it was only a matter of time, and he would be finished off as the bullets hit around him.

As the flare dimmed, Dick crawled a few feet to the northeast. There was just enough light to make out a prone body. He could see Lou's boot. He made his way with painful effort toward Lou's head.

"What happened, Lou?" Dick said.

There was a gurgling sound.

"I'm gonna get you out of here. Hang on, Lou," Dick said near Lou's ear.

There was silence for a brief period. The flare had dimmed further. Dick crawled to his knees and grabbed Lou's belt. He couldn't budge him.

Dick looked toward the coop and saw a weapon report from the southeast corner. He pulled his Smith & Wesson and emptied the gun at the source. Return volleys were directed toward Dick.

Patrick ran to the west side to make sure no one was on that end. He shot a flare toward the northeast to expose whoever was out there. He fired eight rounds from his .22 revolver to draw fire away from Elmer.

Previous flares had ignited the dry grass in the eastern adjacent pasture. Fires spread and grew to an inferno. Flames spread to the northwest, igniting the abandoned house there. Smoke was suffocating, and visibility limited to a few yards.

A barrage of gunfire was directed at Elmer. Patrick grabbed the .45 and directed several shots at gun flashes to the northeast. Patrick turned toward

Elmer, who was curled up in the fetal position. Patrick rushed to him and propped him up. Blood flowed profusely from his chest.

"How bad is it?" Patrick asked.

"It's pretty bad," Elmer said. His voice grew fainter. "We have to get out of here."

Elmer's bleeding increased. Patrick grabbed a head scarf from the bag and tried to stop the bleeding. He feared the worst. "You're not gonna make it if we don't get you out of here," Patrick said. Elmer could not speak. He gasped for breath as blood filled his air duct.

Patrick looked to the south, saw a fence line, and identified a low point. The slope on the south end of the property was steep. Patrick mustered all his strength to pack Elmer on his back and carry their weapons over the fence. Blood flowed from Elmer's chest wound each step of the way. They dropped the .22 and .45 caliber guns. Elmer was lightheaded. "Pat…I gotta lie down. I can't go any farther."

Patrick dragged him to a spot under a grove of trees. It was very dark. Patrick laid him down gently. "Your wound is pretty bad. We've got to get some help."

"I'm done for," Elmer said, gurgling. "Get outta here while you can, Son, before they kill you, too."

"We need to get you some help," Patrick said.

"No, no…I'm done for," Elmer said. "You've got to make a run for it before they take you out, too." Patrick feared his dad was right. Police would kill him if they had the chance. His dad looked bad. There was not much more he could do.

Patrick left his father and headed south and east, climbing toward a ridge to the east. It was hard to see anything. Patrick was exhausted and frightened. Each grinding step over patches of rock and through trees took a toll. Thickets of brush and endless trees blocking cues from the sky clouded his orientation, forcing him to retrace his routes on occasion.

While Patrick and Elmer were making their retreat from the chicken coop, John Dick stayed near Lou, waiting for a break in gunfire and flares shot to expose them. He kept his head down, looking back toward the fence line where the two officers had crossed. "We need backup," Dick yelled as he moved toward the pickup.

The fire spread and turned hot. Dick crawled toward the spot where they had crossed. "Help! Help us! Lou's down!" He stood upright and managed to coax the fence low enough to crawl over it. "Is anybody out there?"

No one responded as the pops and crackles of the fire came closer.

Dick stumbled to the old pickup. "Where in the hell are you? Lou's down. We need backup!" he shouted. The smoke was choking. The heat of the fire was getting closer. Dick fell down. Somehow he managed to right himself and walked toward Cache Creek Road. He stumbled and fell again, looked up, and saw headlights approaching him. Sergeant Carden got out of the car and pulled him to his feet. Dick yelled, "Get the hell up there. Lou's been hit."

Carden moved Dick to the back seat of the police car. Ignoring his plea, Carden drove to a waiting ambulance.

Chapter 7

Fear

Officer Clark, who had remained near his squad car, grabbed his shotgun and crouched in the weeds for cover when he first heard gunshots. He was well to the north of the action near Cache Creek Road. More shots and flares were fired. Clark was convinced he had been targeted. Another flare seemed aimed directly at him.

He ran toward a house to the north across Cache Creek Road, tripping as he tried to cross a ditch. His hand was hurt. He tried to stop blood flowing from his thumb.

Across the road, Sheila Cleveland noticed someone lying in a ditch. She was roused earlier by police cars gathering south of her place, and saw police with flashlights moving toward Elmer's chicken coop. She witnessed the breakout of gunfire and the flares lighting up the sky. As the firefight reached a lull, Cleveland opened her front door and yelled, "Who's out there?"

After yelling a couple of times, Cleveland heard a muffled voice. "I'm Chester Clark, police officer. I've been hit."

"Come up to the house," Cleveland yelled.

There was major bleeding. Cleveland found some towels and cleaned the wound, applied pressure, and stopped the bleeding. "Thanks for helping me," Clark said.

"Glad to be of help. You probably know my brother, John Cleveland, is working as a reserve police officer," Cleveland said.

"Yeah, I know him."

The two looked out the window to see an ambulance moving toward the McGinnis house. Clark ambled toward the EMT, Bill Joseph. He told Joseph he had been hit by gunfire, and his wound was treated.

Roughly two hours after the shooting had ceased, Okanogan Sheriff Deputy Mike Murray arrived at the scene. He was called by tribal dispatch requesting backup at the McGinnis residence. Murray had sketchy details—McGinnis and his son had engaged in a shoot-out with tribal police, one officer was wounded and taken to a local hospital, and another officer was still in the backyard.

Smiskin arrived at the scene around 3:00 a.m. and asked Murray and another deputy named Stevens to secure the area behind the chicken coop before securing the backyard. The fire had spread primarily to the north and east of the McGinnis home. Smoke continued to reduce vision. The two officers circled south of the coop toward a water tower. Someone reported seeing an individual on a water tower south of the McGinnis backyard fence.

The two deputies moved military style, leapfrogging south up a small gully to get a higher view of the water tower. They beamed their lights toward a small recess surrounded by trees and brush, and spotted a man lying prone. When they approached the man, Deputy Stevens aimed his rifle at him. Murray could see a large bloody area between his head and waist. On closer inspection, Murray located a serious wound near his neck. The man was clutching what looked like a pistol. He directed his light toward the weapon, which turned out to be a flare gun.

Seeing that the man's wound was serious, Murray leaned over to see if he was still alive. He yelled "Hello!" a couple of times. The man's eyes opened. Murray asked who he was, and the man identified himself as Elmer McGinnis. "How are you doing?" Murray said.

Elmer said, "I'm a goner."

The pale color of his skin, the coldness of his hand, and the weakness of his voice all led Murray to believe that Elmer's wound was fatal. Murray could see air bubbles spewing from the wound when Elmer tried to talk or breathe. Murray told Elmer that his partner would contact Sergeant Mayo, who was an EMT. They were going to do everything they could to help him.

"Does the house below here belong to you?" asked Murray.

"Yes, that's my home," Elmer struggled to say.

"Can you tell us what happened?"

"When I came home, someone shot at me and I shot back."

Deputy Murray reached for his rights card and read verbatim Elmer's right to remain silent, that anything said could be used against him, and so on. He asked Elmer if he understood each of these rights.

After struggling to get a breath, Elmer answered, "Yes."

"Do you know who shot at the police officers?" Murray asked.

"I don't know—I just shot back."

Sergeant Mayo arrived with a first aid kit. He first examined the chest wound and Elmer's lower-left abdomen, which was saturated with blood. No wound was found in the abdomen area. Mayo cleaned the area around the bullet entry on his upper chest. "Who shot you?" he asked.

"I don't know," Elmer said.

"Who started it?"

"Somebody shot at me and I fired back." Mayo dressed the wound, applying increased compression to stop the bleeding. Elmer added, "I was outside my house behind the chicken coop and there was a stream of light, some kind of beam aimed right at me, and I fired at the light."

"Where's the gun you fired?"

"I dropped the gun in the weeds behind the house."

"Did you have a handgun, and were you standing behind the chicken coop?"

"Yes," Elmer said weakly.

Mayo continued, "So when a light hit you, you fired at that light."

"Yes…I think I hit someone, but not sure who."

"Who was in the house?" Mayo asked.

"I'm not sure…my dogs are there for sure," Elmer said faintly. "Nobody can enter my house unless Laura's there."

"Where is Laura?"

"She's likely in Keller." Elmer's voice grew fainter.

Medics arrived with a stretcher. Elmer's jacket was placed over his body, and he was transported to the Grand Coulee Hospital ER.

More backup deputies arrived after Elmer was located. Chief Smiskin alerted deputies that someone might be inside the McGinnis house, and the chicken coop and backyard had not been cleared.

Deputies who gathered at a nearby barn heard that a shot was fired from the house earlier. Another witness reported seeing a stranger carrying a rifle near Cache Creek Road. A young boy came forward, attracted by all the commotion, and told police he recognized the individual. He said it was Gary Bray. A background check at the Okanogan sheriff's office revealed Bray had done time at Washington Corrections Center at Shelton and was recently released. Police feared Elmer had recruited others like Bray to attack police from the house and possibly hidden sites in the backyard.

Such perceived threats called for more drastic measures. Smiskin contacted the Chelan County SWAT team and requested help to secure the area. The SWAT team, based in Wenatchee, immediately gathered to make the 115-mile trip to the scene.

While waiting for the SWAT team, Toney Fitzhugh, chief criminal deputy for the Okanogan County Sheriff's Department, set about to secure the backyard. With other officers providing cover for Fitzhugh, tear gas was fired at the McGinnis house. The first shot did not break through the window. The second round penetrated. Smoke billowed from the broken window. Officers waited with guns aimed at the entrance of the house. After waiting for nearly a half hour, no one emerged.

The intense fires to the east and north had not abated. Smoke still limited clear vision of the backyard and the McGinnis house.

The chicken house had yet to be cleared. Fitzhugh cautiously opened every cage door, one at a time, then moved to the rear of the chicken coop and found no one. As the morning sun made its appearance to the east, Fitzhugh made out through the smoke to the east what appeared to be an officer on the ground. He made his way in military combat fashion toward the prone body.

As a precaution, he took cover behind a concrete foundation. Seeing no one in the area, he crawled toward the downed officer. He checked for a pulse in his left wrist. There was no pulse. The officer's hand was cold. His joints were stiff. Rigor mortis had set in.

Sergeant Millard was at last reached. The officer was downed by a fatal bullet that struck just above his Second Chance bulletproof vest.

Police still had not entered the McGinnis house. The Chelan SWAT team finally arrived around 6:30 a.m. After discussing the situation with officers on the scene, the SWAT captain made a tactical decision to rush the McGinnis house. They kicked the door open. About five SWAT members entered, ready for the worst—other assailants or booby traps.

Elmer's dogs barked and rushed toward the SWAT team. Officers took direct aim at the dogs with 9-millimeter handguns and a shotgun. All the dogs were killed. An escaping dog was gunned down as the animal made its way toward the chicken coop.

Even though the SWAT team was inside the house and Elmer's dogs had been killed, police remained edgy. Officers feared someone might be in an underground tunnel.

Much later that morning, FBI agent Jim Davis took charge of the investigation. He arrived a little before 10:00 a.m. Minutes after his arrival, Agent Davis reported hearing a gunshot, possibly from the basement of the McGinnis house. Someone had told him the house had a basement or tunnel, which later turned out to be untrue. Others on the scene failed to confirm the agent's report.

Chapter 8

Refuge

Jeffery Epperson, a friend of Patrick Hoffman, first heard about the shoot-out in Nespelem from his wife. Her sister had called to warn her not to go through Nespelem. Police had cordoned off Cache Creek Road near Elmer McGinnis's house.

The Eppersons' home was in Keller, roughly twenty miles east of Nespelem, just north of a small lake and the Keller post office. It was nestled behind the Catholic church, Rosa of Lima. (Historically, Jesuits established churches in most villages in the Okanogan and Kettle Falls region, along with an Indian school.)

Jeff headed out the door to shoe some horses. Fred Leskinen had called Jeff that morning and said he needed some help with horses at Dave Nee's barn. Dave was a neighbor who took good care of his horses, and Fred loved raising and breeding horses; Jeff had agreed to give Dave a hand. The two worked together and shared their farrier business profits.

While shoeing the horses, Fred chided Jeff. "Pat Hoffman is likely headed for your place, looking for help and a hideout."

"Is that a joke? I sure hope so," Jeff laughed.

≢ ≢ ≢

Over the steep terrain along the way to Keller, Patrick Hoffman increased his pace, fearful police were closing in on him. Working through brush and navigating the talus slopes sapped his energy. It had taken over a day to reach the summit. He faced a long descent into the San Poil Valley. Patrick was cold, hungry, and scared. Perhaps police had brought in their dogs to track him, or were doing an air search. He didn't know.

After a sleepless night of trying to stay warm, Patrick made his way to the San Poil Valley. There was a break in the ponderosas, allowing him to see the highway and find his way to the back door of Jeffrey Epperson's house. Patrick and his buddy Jeff partied and did some target shooting together. Patrick was very tired. Maybe Jeff would provide relief and a way to avoid police.

Jeff and Fred returned to the Epperson house around 2:00 p.m. They sat down with Jeff's wife at the kitchen table for coffee and a chat. The couple's youngest boy came running up the hallway from the back door. "Somebody wants to talk with you, Dad."

For Jeff, this seemed odd. Visitors rarely ever came to the back door. Their entrance faced the only arterial in Keller, State Route 21. His son persisted. "Dad, you better come look." Thinking his son may have had heard Fred and him joke over Pat Hoffman showing up, Jeff told his son he was tired of the Pat Hoffman jokes. To be safe, Jeff went to the back door anyway.

Jeff Epperson was astounded. There Pat Hoffman stood at the back door. He had a pair of Levi's covering dirty cowboy boots and a gray coat tied around his waist.

To Jeff, Pat looked very frightened. His hair and beard were long, but still exposed scratches on his face. Jeff focused on Patrick's intense eyes, thinking he was just like a penned colt, not knowing where to go next. He didn't have the look of a bad man, Jeff thought, only someone who really needed help. "Do you have any weapons with you?" Jeff asked.

"No. I need to talk," Patrick said.

Jeff invited Pat onto the back porch. Fred nodded at Pat. Fred had pastured some of his horses with Laura's pony at the McGinnis spread.

"What happened?" Jeff asked.

"Dad was shot and killed. I had to get away before they killed me, too," Patrick said, his eyes still dilated.

"You got that wrong. Elmer wasn't killed. Your dad was shot, but he's alive. He's in a hospital," Jeff said. He showed Pat a local paper and pointed out the story. "They managed to get Elmer out in time and patch him up."

Patrick scanned the paper to get the details.

Jeff pointed out, "A couple police were shot. Lou Millard was killed."

"Good deal," Patrick said.

Patrick seemed to calm a little but remained tense. "I know if they track me down, they will kill me."

"That won't work for you to stay here. I can't expose my family," Jeff said. "You've got to go. I've got to protect my family."

"Maybe I'll head north—maybe Canada," Patrick said.

"Running is no solution. You need to give yourself up," Jeff said.

Patrick thought it over. "How about a ride to Sam Miller's place just up the valley?"

"I can't do that, Pat. There's no point in getting other people involved," Jeff said. "The best solution is to surrender to police."

Patrick looked away.

"Wait here on the back porch while I talk this over with my wife," Jeff said.

Patrick nodded.

Jeff revealed his fears to his wife. It was best they pack the kids and go elsewhere as long as Pat was around. Jeff drove the family to a neighbor's house and returned shortly.

Fred remained with Patrick on the back porch. "There's really only one option, Pat. If you want to stop the killing, you've got to go with Jeff's suggestion and turn yourself in if you want our help."

"I don't trust any cops at this point. They'll gun me down on sight," Patrick said.

Jeff joined the two on the porch and repeated his argument that Pat should turn himself in.

"There's no way I'll surrender to tribal police. They'll shoot first and ask later," Patrick said.

"What about turning yourself in to a federal marshal or the FBI or even the Ferry County sheriff?" Jeff said.

"No way. I don't trust any of them," Patrick said.

Fred suggested, "Why not call Johnny Johnston? He would be fair." Patrick had known the Okanogan County sheriff when Johnston served on the tribal police force.

Patrick thought about it and did not respond immediately. He paced a step or two and looked out the porch door toward the yard. Patrick looked back at Fred and nodded.

With Pat's nod, Fred said, "Good. Let's give it a try."

Jeff called Johnny Johnston and put Patrick on the phone. "I'm willing to make my way to your office if you can guarantee my safety," Patrick said.

Johnston made it clear he was to arrive unarmed and surrender peacefully. "You'll be safe once you turn yourself in. You have my word," Johnston said.

The three piled into Fred's pickup. "What if someone recognizes you?" asked Jeff.

"You're right on. We don't want to get in any shoot-out with cops," Fred said. The only route to the sheriff's office was over Cache Creek Road.

"My wife said the McGinnis place is surrounded with police," Jeff said. "There could be a roadblock."

Fred had a pair of sunglasses, an extra ball cap, and a polka-dotted cowboy shirt in the truck. "Put this cap on—see how it fits," Fred said. "You look a little different, but let's try these sunglasses and a different shirt." Patrick changed shirts and tried the sunglasses for fit. "Unless they really get close, I think you'll pass," Fred said. "Be sure to keep that cap pulled down."

"You look like the real deal, like a wrangler who's gone bad on his luck and even lost his hat," Jeff said with a smile.

No one had much money. Fred had just gotten his check for shoeing the horses. Pat had a little cash, around twenty-five bucks. It was money he had set aside to give his sisters for food and other incidentals. Fred asked if they might borrow the money and pay him back when the horseshoe check was cashed.

Fred gassed up the truck. There was enough left to buy each a burger and a Coke. On the way to Okanogan, Pat told Jeff more of what happened at the McGinnis place. "How did it start?" Jeff asked.

"There were lights shining at the corner of the chicken coop, and the lights hit us. There was no 'hands up,' no 'halt' or nothing, and then the shooting started," Patrick said. "The police shot first, and then they fired flares at us. We were behind the chicken coop when it all broke out. After a few shots, Dad got hit."

"Did you shoot back?" Jeff asked.

"Yes, we had to defend ourselves."

"So, what did you use as a weapon?"

"I had the forty-five and the twenty-two. I fired them into the ground and into the air to keep the officers back, to help Dad."

"What about the 9-millimeter?" Jeff said.

"Elmer had the 9-millimeter," Patrick said.

"Did he fire it?" Fred asked.

"Yes. He had to defend himself," Patrick said.

"So what happened to the 9-millimeter?" Jeff asked. Jeff had done target shooting with Patrick and had fired several rounds with the weapon.

"I helped Dad get to safety after being hit. We had some cover with the smoke and all to get to a clearing," Patrick said. "I really thought Dad was dying. He was struggling to get a breath."

"What did you do with the 9-millimeter?" Jeff persisted.

"I dropped it on the way up the ridge after leaving Dad. I got rid of it—stashed it on the way up the hill. It was getting too heavy to pack," Patrick clarified.

Fred slowed his pickup as the threesome made their way past the eerie inferno scene of the shoot-out.

"I wonder if the horses survived?" asked Jeff.

"Look…that old abandoned house burned clear down to the foundation," Fred said.

Patrick said little as he bent over to hide his face.

Fred made an exit from town. He kept the pickup under the speed limit over Disautel Pass to the sheriff's office. No police were encountered en route to the parking lot of the Okanogan County Sheriff's Office. Patrick showed up as promised. Sheriff Johnston took him into custody. Patrick Hoffman could relax a little. He now felt safe.

Chapter 9

Charges

Elmer's wound was stitched over. His strength grew daily over a week in the hospital. The treatment team agreed his condition had improved such that he could be released to federal authorities and treated in a federal facility in Spokane, Washington.

A board on the corner of the chicken coop and a snap at the top of his shirt had slowed the deadly velocity of the bullet that hit him. The deflections spared his life. The slug entered beneath his larynx and traveled obliquely through his chest, ending in his right arm. Leaving the bullet in place was not considered critical.

Patrick remained in the Okanogan County Jail awaiting a transfer. FBI Agent Davis and BIA Agent Al Aubertin chartered a private plane to pick up Patrick and fly him to Spokane for possible federal charges. The agents and Patrick remained silent as the pilot powered the small aircraft to a safe altitude to cross mountainous terrain. As they approached Spokane, Patrick peered out of the window, surveying the Columbia Plateau landscape. In a pensive moment, not really addressing anyone, Patrick said, "Everything just seemed to erupt...I didn't think it would turn out this way."

District Attorney Earl Hicks wasted no time getting to the crime scene. He wanted to see for himself what had happened. Seeing the burnt fields and foundation of what was once a house, and reviewing the evidence, Hicks told officers on the scene, "Lou Millard will not go down in vain for doing his duty as a tribal police officer."

Thirteen days after the incident, Hicks filed first-degree murder charges against Elmer McGinnis and Patrick Hoffman. A federal grand jury was summoned. Two days later, the jury was brought together in the federal courthouse to determine whether the defendants should be indicted.

Hicks opened his case against Elmer McGinnis and Patrick Hoffman by stating that a violent father and his son, acting as an accomplice, attacked police during the early morning hours of August 27, 1986. "The evidence will show that the defendants willfully engaged in an attack on tribal police attempting to make a lawful arrest," Hicks said. "Defendants Elmer McGinnis and Patrick Hoffman repeatedly assaulted police with gunfire, resulting in the tragic death of Sergeant Louis Millard and wounding of Assistant Chief John Dick. We will show that such actions constitute crimes of first-degree murder and criminal assault."

Hicks called Jim Davis as a witness. Davis was based in Spokane, Washington, and had been with the bureau over twenty years. He had previously investigated crimes on reservations in eastern Washington and knew most of the officers at the scene of the shootings. "What physical evidence did you find at the crime scene?" Hicks said.

"First of all, I want to point out that we used a matrix approach to search areas around the defendant's house," Davis said. "We marked off the scene with flags every three feet, and in a criss-cross fashion we searched along those sight lines for bullets, spent flare cartridges, brass, and weapons."

"Tell the jury what you found." Hicks said.

"A forty-five-caliber automatic was located near a bush not far from a chicken coop in McGinnis's backyard. Brass from the forty-five was found nearby at the southeastern corner of the coop. We found three loaded forty-five clips and one that was empty."

"What else did you find?" asked the prosecutor.

"Two 9-millimeter casings were found behind the chicken coop." Davis brought forward an aerial photo showing the chicken coop and pointed out where the casings were located, midway behind the coop.

"Could you determine if a weapon or weapons were fired from this position?"

"We investigated the angle of shots from the chicken coop to Sergeant Millard's flashlight. We located a bullet hole in a tree trunk behind the flashlight. Given the location of the flashlight and bullet hole, the angle of the shot lined up with the shooter firing from the chicken coop."

"What did you conclude as to the likely source of the fatal bullet that was directed at Sergeant Millard?"

"Based on location of the brass and angle of shots fired from the chicken coop, I concluded it was a 9-millimeter weapon. A K-99 assault pistol the defendants had at the scene was used to kill Millard."

"Were you able to establish that the defendants had a 9-millimeter weapon in their possession the morning of August twenty-seventh?" asked Hicks.

"Yes. Francis Peoples, the daughter of Elmer McGinnis, was interviewed by FBI Agent Burke after the shoot-out. She acknowledged Patrick Hoffman regularly carried a K-99 assault pistol in his gym bag. Peoples said Hoffman had possession of the bag when the defendants were last seen exiting Lila McGinnis's car at Armstrong Meadows. When Elmer exited the car, he warned his daughters that they needed to stay out of the line of fire."

Agent Davis testified that Elmer and Patrick made their way from Armstrong Meadows to a hill outside the McGinnis house. "The defendants made a dash across Cache Creek Road. A tribal officer, Officer Phillips, who was watching the place to the east, saw two men crossing Cache Creek Road. The gym bag was carried some six miles over backcountry to the crime scene. We found the black gym bag behind the chicken coop."

"What actions did tribal police take when first arriving at the entrance to the McGinnis property?" Hicks asked.

"At about two-ten a.m., as indicated on dispatch logs, John Dick and

Louis Millard, along with another officer, Gary Carden, approached two abandoned houses north of the McGinnis house to see if anyone was around. Officers Dick and Millard, after checking the houses, headed south past the McGinnis house along a barbed-wire fence on the east property line approaching the McGinnis backyard. The two officers climbed over the fence and proceeded toward the chicken coop."

"Did Sergeant Carden join them?" Hicks asked.

"No. Carden approached the McGinnis place from the west property line by walking up a drive and around a parked van in the driveway."

"What did Officers Millard and Dick do next?"

"Dick and Millard walked toward a woodpile, shined a light on it, and then saw a chicken coop. Dick decided to walk behind the coop to see if there was a door open."

"Could the officer see anyone?" asked Hicks.

"No, he didn't. Dick reported somebody could have been lying on the ground or the top of the coop and he wouldn't have seen them," Davis said.

"What did Officer Dick do next?"

"No doors were open, so Dick turned around and walked back toward Millard. Dick reported seeing a flash over his left shoulder and hearing a loud noise. He felt something hit the back of his shoulder. He realized he had been shot. He yelled to Millard, 'I'm hit,' and Millard hollered back, 'If you're hit, get on the ground.' Dick dropped to the ground. As he fell, the officer could see another volley of shots fired toward them. Dick reported that he believed his partner Millard shot his gun at this time."

"Was there evidence Sergeant Millard had fired his revolver?" asked Hicks.

"Yes, we found two empty rounds in Millard's pistol."

"What did tribal officers observe when shooting broke out?"

"Carden said he heard someone yell 'halt' or something like that before the first shot was fired. Carden was behind the van when it all broke out. He did not draw his weapon or fire it."

"Why didn't Carden respond?"

"Carden had no idea who was shooting or where the shooting was coming from."

"Where was the officer hit—Officer Dick, that is?"

"The doctor who treated him concluded the entry definitely was in the back and exited the front near Dick's armpit," Davis said. "The bullet was likely a .45, low-velocity weapon as opposed to a .38 or a 9-millimeter bullet that travels faster and is smaller."

The prosecutor asked, "What did tribal officers report as to what they heard or saw when shooting broke out?"

"Carden reported he heard a shot, followed by a rapid firing of four or five shots that were louder than later shots. The later shots were from a larger caliber gun," Davis said.

"Where was Officer Millard wounded during the shoot-out?"

"Millard was hit just above his flak jacket protection, penetrating his lung, resulting in considerable bleeding. He struggled to get to his feet after being hit, but couldn't make it."

"Did you find the murder weapon?"

"We did a search for the 9-millimeter weapon in a twenty-five mile area between Nespelem and Keller. The terrain was very difficult to search due to considerable brush and trees and the steepness of the ridge. We brought in a helicopter to gain an aerial perspective of likely routes Patrick Hoffman may have used. In addition, dogs were used in the search to find any potential scent. A subsequent rain reduced chances of finding the route. The 9-millimeter weapon was never found."

Hicks ended his examination by asking Davis, "What remarks did Patrick Hoffman make to his friend Jeffrey Epperson about who fired the 9-millimeter weapon?"

"Epperson said Elmer McGinnis had possession of the K-99 and had fired it. When he heard that Louis Millard had been killed, Hoffman said to Epperson, 'Good deal.'"

In later testimony, Davis cited Patrick Hoffman's remark on the flight to Spokane: "Everything just seemed to erupt… I didn't think it would turn out this way." Davis concluded that the passing remark revealed Hoffman had anticipated doing battle with police. After a few more questions covering the SWAT team's raid, Hicks dismissed his key witness.

Hicks summarized the case against the defendants. "There is no question Elmer McGinnis and Patrick Hoffman showed deadly intent. When police appeared, the defendants fired multiple rounds at officers, including flares to expose their location. Elmer McGinnis anticipated a battle with tribal police and warned his daughters to stay out of the line of fire.

"As for Patrick Hoffman, he, too, anticipated and prepared to do battle with police. He carried a gym bag containing three firearms and a flare gun over miles of backcountry to the scene of the crime."

The grand jury met and reached a decision after a few hours. Elmer McGinnis and Patrick Hoffman were indicted for first-degree murder. Earl Hicks filed charges in federal district court with Judge Quackenbush presiding.

Chapter 10

Finding a Judge for the Trial

At the same time the grand jury was summoned for murder charges, Hicks was negotiating with Okanogan County Prosecutor Doug Boole to consider shifting jurisdiction of the trial to a state court, Okanogan Superior Court. The defendants were arraigned for the murder charges in federal district court on September 12. Judge Quackenbush insisted that Elmer McGinnis undergo a psychiatric evaluation before setting bail. The judge was particularly concerned about the potential danger of allowing McGinnis to be at large.

Jeffrey Burnside, a Spokane KREM television news reporter, made a call to the federal holding facility to request an interview with Elmer McGinnis. Elmer was contacted and returned a call to Burnside.

Burnside identified himself and said, "I'd like to do a taped interview. Is that okay with you?"

"Yes. The truth of this whole thing needs to be brought out," Elmer said.

"Would it be okay to do an interview this morning, say an hour from now?" Burnside asked.

"Sure," Elmer said.

Burnside arrived shortly at the facility with a cameraman. "How did it start?" asked Burnside.

"We were ambushed by police, who opened fire from twelve different positions, firing between sixty and eighty shots at us," Elmer said. "They fired multiple flares at us to flush us out."

"Did you fire any flares?" asked the reporter.

"Yes, I just fired one shot."

"Did you shoot any other weapons?"

"No. I didn't fire any weapon," Elmer said calmly.

"How did it all start?"

"I was hit by the first shot. I first noticed a red dot or light coming at me, say eighteen to twenty feet away and about ten to twelve inches off the ground, and then this red dot hit my body and shrank to the size of about a nickel. That is when I was shot."

"Who shot the officer, Sergeant Millard?"

"I think it was police who hit him during the crossfire."

"Was anyone with you?"

"I was the only one on the property that night," Elmer said.

The fifteen-minute taped interview was reduced to less than a minute, and aired over a good part of Eastern Washington that evening and next.

On October 29, 1986, Judge R. J. McNichols of the federal district court replaced Judge Quackenbush to conduct the trial. The first witness, Dr. Cressey, was called to the stand to offer his psychiatric assessment of Elmer McGinnis.

The experienced forensic psychiatrist focused on the question of competency and dangerousness. Dr. Cressey testified the defendant was competent to stand trial. He told the court that when he first met Elmer McGinnis on September 15, he had not anticipated his medical condition. "I saw Mr. McGinnis at the Spokane County Jail. I didn't realize what kind of physical shape he was in until I walked in the holding area," Cressey said. "He was wearing a robe, sitting in a wheelchair, and he had a scabbed-over area right below his neckline. It was a red spot that I thought looked like a hole. I didn't realize he had been wounded.

"Elmer McGinnis appeared complacent about his confinement. When I asked, 'Are you making any plans to seek bail from the court?' Mr. McGinnis told me, 'No way. I'm just fine here. There's no way I'd set foot in Nespelem. It's too dangerous.' When I asked, 'Why do you say it is dangerous?' he said, 'They're going to finish the job if I walk out of here.' I asked him, 'Who's *they*?' and McGinnis answered, 'It's the tribal police. They're out to do a hit job on me and my boy over what we know.'"

"He told me the council and the police were as rotten as skunk cabbage, that both the Colville Business Council and the tribal police had been taking money under the table for years. He claimed to have evidence to show anyone this is true. I pressed Mr. McGinnis about his allegations to determine if he was experiencing psychotic delusions or hallucinations. I also explored Mr. McGinnis's orientation as to person, place, and time. Based on these assessments, I found no evidence of psychosis or dementia," Cressey concluded. "But Elmer did manifest a paranoid personality disorder."

Dr. Cressey summarized his findings to the court. "Elmer McGinnis showed no psychosis and readily understood what others said and did. As to the question of dangerousness to others, that seems to be a moot question for the court since Elmer has declined to seek bail."

The judge suspended setting bail pending a motion for change of venue.

Hicks made a venue-change motion for the federal court to dismiss the charges without prejudice and remand the case to Okanogan County Superior Court. Defense attorneys objected, pointing out the Colville Reservation was the creation of the federal government, and in that light jurisdiction should remain in federal court. Hicks argued that the very fact the reservation was created by government had allowed the State of Washington to negotiate a settlement over jurisdiction directly with the Colville Business Council. In this case, the council voted in 1964 to remand jurisdiction to the State of Washington. After hearing arguments, Judge McNichols granted the dismissal and the case was remanded to state court.

"All charges will be dropped in the Eastern District Federal Court without prejudice," declared the judge. The option remained that the case could be referred back to a federal court if further charges were to be considered.

Five days earlier, Prosecutor Boole had filed aggravated first-degree murder charges against Elmer McGinnis and Patrick Hoffman in Okanogan County Superior Court. The court was just a few miles west of the reservation boundary some forty-two miles west of Nespelem.

Superior Court Judge Jim Thomas heard the arraignment. The judge had a reputation of making tough calls based on a fair reading of the law. As a judge, he was old school. His rulings were handwritten rather than relying on boilerplate language outlined in previous case law. In this one-judge county, the defendants faced a politically conservative jurist. Jim Thomas had served as prosecutor earlier in his career and left for a private practice. A successful law practice led to a partnership with Joseph Wicks, who headed the firm and was a former judge. Wicks had been elected for three terms as judge in Okanogan and Ferry Counties beginning in 1946. Wicks was enrolled in the Cherokee Nation in Oklahoma. Wicks's daughter Ann met Jim Thomas in college, and they married in 1956.

During the defendants' October 24 arraignment, arguments were made as to whether either should be granted bail. Judge Thomas listened to Prosecutor Boole's arguments that each defendant was dangerous and at risk to flee. The judge also reviewed defense arguments that the defendants had no intention to leave the country. Without comment, bail was set at half a million dollars for each.

After their arraignment, Prosecutor Boole had second thoughts about Judge Thomas hearing the case. Boole filed an affidavit of prejudice against Judge Thomas. By law, Judge Thomas was forced to step down from the trial. The affidavit was unexpected and unprecedented. County prosecutors statewide rarely filed an affidavit against a sitting judge.

Elmer reacted strongly to the news. "It's all about the judge being married to a Cherokee," he complained to his court-appointed attorney, Scot Stuart. "Boole wants a hanging judge. Well, damnit, do something to stop them."

Patrick agreed. "We're getting a bad deal being in state court in the first place, and now they take out a judge who they thought would listen to us," he complained to his attorney.

"How can this prosecutor dictate who's the judge in this case?" Elmer said.

Stuart outlined Washington law on removal of judges—either party can file an affidavit of prejudice against a judge without citing any reason in the motion.

"What's good for the goose is good for the gander. By God, we have the same right as I see it," Elmer said.

A week later the Washington State Court administration office appointed a substitute judge from Grant County, Judge Evan Sperline. Elmer insisted his attorney file an affidavit of prejudice against the new judge. Stuart complied and filed the affidavit. A substitute judge from Ferry County was appointed, Judge Stewart. Patrick followed suit by filing an affidavit against the new appointee.

It was up to the Court Administration Office, a branch of the Washington State Supreme Court, to appoint a substitute judge. On November 25, staff contacted my wife, Jo Anne Alumbaugh, a judge from Kittitas County, and asked if she would hear the case. A state supreme court judge was put on the phone to discuss the appointment. The judge, who remained unidentified, expressed concern over the number of affidavits of prejudice filed against Judge Alumbaugh and the growing backlog of cases in her home court.

Still reeling from her 1984 election victory, bitter local bar members had prevented Jo Anne from hearing virtually any of their cases. Perhaps if she agreed to take the case the justice offered, her backlog could be reduced by a substitute judge during what was expected to be a lengthy trial.

Judge Alumbaugh contacted Judge Thomas to discuss a possible swap to cover Kittitas County during the trial. Judge Thomas agreed to these arrangements even though he, too, was worried about a backlog of cases in the Okanogan County building in his absence. This was the price of serving in one-judge counties.

My wife accepted the appointment. The next day she contacted the

Okanogan prosecutor's office and the county court administrator to determine the earliest date a pretrial hearing could be held. She called the defense attorneys to discuss possible pretrial dates. Attorneys emphasized that a large number of pretrial motions had yet to be heard. Prosecutors and defense attorneys faced a deadline to have their motions heard. The sixty-day rule adopted by Washington courts required the trial date be set no more than sixty days after arraignment. The judge reminded all parties that such a constraint meant the trial would begin December 29.

Chapter 11

Home Court Disadvantage

Attorneys agreed to set the first pretrial for December 3, 1986. My wife agreed to have me drive her on the wintry day over Blewett Pass to the Okanogan County Courthouse. The high bluffs created by a massive fault along the Columbia River reminded me of another potential fault line. I wondered what she possibly would face during this trial. Had it been worth it? Breaking glass ceilings to be a judge had taken a toll. Now, she had yet another hurdle to add to her stressful tenure.

Jo Anne Alumbaugh was the first woman to practice law in Kittitas County and the first woman to be elected as a superior court judge east of the Cascades. Her rise to the position of judge had been anything but easy, yet she felt pride in finally being in a position to initiate court reforms she had proposed during the campaign.

Her path to a law career was largely sparked by efforts to bring about local juvenile reform. During the 1970s, Jo Anne joined other women activists, many from the Kittitas League of Women Voters, to support statewide reform on the treatment of juveniles. At the time, dependents such as runaways and incorrigible youth were prosecuted in juvenile court just as delinquents were. Too often, dependents and delinquents were denied due process. Ultimately, the local League combined with statewide lobbyists and persuaded Washington legislators to pass the 1977 State Juvenile Reform Act.

The reform act addressed many of the local concerns of League members in Kittitas County. However, the local judge, Superior Court Judge R. Bob Cole, who had served for two decades in that position with support of county commissioners, pushed back on the reform provisions of the bill. Most vexing to League members, Judge Cole and his juvenile officer Ike Hamblin routinely detained runaway youth and juvenile delinquents charged with crimes along with adults in the county jail. Over a period of three years, the League contacted the judge and commissioners to seek ways that the county could enforce separate detention and protect juveniles from potential abuse by adult inmates. Judge Cole held firm, as did Hamblin and Sheriff Bob Barrett, their argument essentially that youth must be held accountable for their behavior and suffer the consequences.

League members contacted a Seattle attorney, Rick Blumberg, and asked what options they had. He recommended filing a complaint in federal court. Following his advice and counsel, the Kittitas League of Women Voters filed a lawsuit against Kittitas County, charging that civil rights of juveniles had been violated.

Blumberg met with Kittitas Prosecutor David Gorrie to see if a pretrial accord could be reached. The two attorneys debated applicable federal law and potential consequences of the suit. Seeing that defense of the suit was a no-win outcome for the county, Gorrie agreed to the terms offered by Blumberg. The lawsuit would be dropped if Kittitas County agreed to detain juveniles in a separate facility. Politically, it was a bittersweet victory for League members.

To locals, including the sheriff and the judge, the debate was really over the parents' role in raising their children. Reformers pushing the Juvenile Reform Act were too soft on misbehaving juveniles, undercutting family rearing practices. In their view, juveniles who abandoned their families needed to experience the harsh realities of behaviors leading to a criminal lifestyle.

Such views were underscored at the Washington State Conference on Women held in Ellensburg, Washington, on July 8, 1977. Roughly four thousand women and a few husbands attended. Supporters of pro-family values voiced their complaints that equal rights for women had led to abortion and gay rights. In addition, pro-feminist values were responsible for neglectful families, which were overrepresented in cases of youth alienation, drug abuse, and delinquency. Their views on reform of women's rights carried the day. Women activists supporting the Equal Rights Amendment were loudly shouted down during the debate. Conservative women representing Mormon, Catholic, and evangelical faiths carried the day and voted down the ERA.

Jo Anne Alumbaugh was not about to throw in the towel after the conference. She complained to other activists that action was needed, not one more study group discussing the need for social change.

On one sunny April afternoon, Jo Anne asked that I meet her in our bedroom for a chat away from our son and daughter. Without explanation she said starkly, "I'm leaving." I was stunned for a moment.

"Does this mean it's over?" I asked.

"No...but I am going to law school. You can stay here if you must."

Breaking up our family was out of the question. Job security was secondary to keeping us together. I thought of options that evening. The next morning I offered my resignation to the chair of the psychology department, John Silva. John asked that I reconsider, that Central Washington University was developing programs off campus, and there might be opportunities for full-time faculty placement.

The appointment was offered, and the next fall I took a full-time position serving three West Side campus programs for working adults returning for higher degrees.

We moved to Tacoma, Washington. Two years later Jo Anne completed her law degree at the University of Puget Sound, taking extra law courses during the summer of 1978. She passed the bar exam and we returned to Ellensburg, where she did a brief stint in the prosecutor's office. Her goals for legal reform had not been forgotten. Jo Anne began a solo practice in the historic 1888 building in Ellensburg. A growing practice developed with a variety of clients, including youth and women in abusive relationships.

As the first woman to practice law in Kittitas County, Jo Anne experienced a few bruising encounters with local attorneys. That was expected. Women lawyer friends from Seattle, Tacoma, and Olympia urged her to stay the course and establish her own niche in domestic and juvenile law. Feedback from clients also gave her encouragement. They were pleased to find an independent voice who dealt with their concerns directly, fairly, and effectively.

Judge R. Bob Cole was up for reelection in the fall of 1984. Having served on the bench for twenty-seven years, the judge was expected to win his next term. Bar members privately expressed their desire to challenge the incumbent, but none stepped forward.

At literally the last hour for filing, Jo Anne, who had just turned forty-two, filed for the position. Reactions were predictable. Few bar members took her candidacy seriously, including Judge Cole.

In Ellensburg, activists for local juvenile reform helped organize a grassroots campaign for the challenger. Campaigners addressed envelopes for a two-page letter that was sent to all registered county voters. The letter outlined her proposed juvenile and domestic court reforms. Campaign volunteers included local League members, faculty from Central Washington University, college students, and a number of local and rural residents seeking an independent candidate for judge.

Campaign rallies were held throughout Kittitas County. Most residents, including those in remote rural areas, were doorbelled. The campaign theme, "It's Time for a Change," caught on with voters, who put up signs over much of the county.

Jo Anne won the primary. Since she would have been the only candidate placed on the general ballot, her election for the bench was considered pro forma by precedent. However, attorneys supporting Judge Cole saw it differently.

Her primary win shocked most observers, including the editor of the local paper, the *Ellensburg Daily Record*, and most decidedly Kittitas County bar members. The Kittitas Bar Association wasted little time. Bar members gathered to consider options for the general election. Members opted to promote a write-in candidacy for the chair of Judge Cole's financial campaign, attorney Bob Fraser.

The campaign turned personal. Accusations of lying and questions of competency generated print and media attention. Virtually all local attorneys supported Bob Fraser. Ten attorneys signed an ad that declared they were ethically obligated as attorneys to protest judges unfit or incompetent to serve.

Bob Fraser and his supporters anticipated a larger voter turnout for the general election with Ronald Reagan running for a second term. Voters who had not voted in the primary were expected to be swayed by attorney recommendations and reverse the primary outcome.

Voters clearly were energized over the give and take of the ensuing campaign. Letters to the editor protested strongly that attorneys had deemed the elected judge incompetent before hearing a case in court. One letter stood out, saying, "A woman has to do twice as well to be thought half as good."

On the eve of the general election, attorneys and supporters of the write-in candidate ran a full-page ad in the *Ellensburg Daily Record* displaying a full-page photo of Bob Fraser with a stern look, surrounded by law books in the background, with the caption: "You May Need a <u>Good</u> Judge Someday."

Voter turnout for the judicial race was high. Clearly Kittitas voters had followed the debate and made their decision. Jo Anne Alumbaugh won convincingly with a record vote total.

Activist women in the community celebrated. At last, the first woman judge had been elected east of the Cascades. When a reporter asked Bob Fraser if he would appear before the new judge, he said, "I don't know if I can take my clients there or not…I doubt it."

Attorneys took their cue. A January headline in the *Record* read, "New Judge Faces Flood of Affidavits." Jo Anne had yet to be sworn in, and 101 affidavits of prejudice had already been filed against her. Who filed them? How were they counted? The article provided none of these details.

Disgruntled attorneys made their feelings known. Her victory was a fluke. Voters were ill informed as to the qualifications of the two candidates. She was inexperienced and incompetent. Yes, the new judge had only been in practice five years before her election, but the major issue was gender, or so it seemed to her supporters. As Heather Coughlin, editor of the *CWU Observer*, pointed out, "The 'Good Ol' Boys Party' insisted on having one of their own to preserve their friendly relationships with the court."

For the next two years, the attorney boycott continued. Judge Alumbaugh may have been ahead of her time on issues of gender equality and court reforms for domestic cases, but the stigma of being accused of incompetency slowed her efforts toward these aims. Was she fit to be judge?

Chapter 12

Rocky First Day

Gaveling the December 3 pretrial to order, Judge Alumbaugh struggled to adjust the oversized chair. Failing to find the right height, she looked up and addressed the attorneys. "Good morning." As she struggled to elevate her chair, Elmer and Patrick shook their heads in despair.

The judge found the right lever and adjusted the chair's height to more easily read motions for the day. "Let's get to the pretrial hearing for today," she said, turning to the defendants. "Both you, Elmer McGinnis, and you, Patrick Hoffman, have been charged with aggravated first-degree murder and assault of tribal officers Louis Millard and John Dick, respectively. The purpose of the pretrial hearing is to determine what evidence will be allowed during the trial and to resolve any procedural matters as to how the trial will be conducted."

Elmer could hardly restrain himself. His stare at the new judge was hard to ignore as his attorney remained focused on the pending motions. Elmer's arousal intensified. This was the fourth judge in what was becoming a circus. His hand tremored. He paid little attention to his attorney, Owen M. "Bud" Gardner.

"This is bullshit!" Elmer yelled.

Gardner grabbed Elmer's arm and insisted he calm down. Patrick was equally defiant with a menacing glare toward the judge. He said little.

Elmer's outburst did not divert the judge. "Let's proceed to the matters at hand."

"This is total and complete bullshit." Elmer was not about to be constrained. How could he be tried in this court for anything? A federal judge said charges had been dismissed.

Elmer misunderstood, or more likely parsed, Judge McNichols' ruling, even though Gardner had explained its meaning. Dismissing charges in federal court only applied to the federal court, and did not mean that charges would be dropped by the state. Elmer ignored the advice of his attorney. "By God," he said, "dismissal meant dismissal."

Elmer had doubts, as with previous judges, that this one would conduct a fair hearing. What did she know about Indian law?

Both defendants had parted ways with previous court-appointed attorneys, dismayed over the handling of their defense. Before handling their case, Judge Stewart had approved substitute attorneys: Owen Gardner for Elmer and R. John Sloan Jr. for Patrick.

John Sloan stepped forward and requested that the judge consider his motion for increased funding for representation before moving to the substantive pretrial motions. "Funds are needed to hire an assistant and fees for expert witnesses," he said. "This case involves a myriad of legal issues that will require a significant number of attorney hours. The case could swamp my representation for other clients."

The court paid forty dollars an hour, but Sloan's rate was typically seventy-five dollars an hour. He pointed out that other attorneys charged more, up to ninety dollars an hour, for such cases. Sloan claimed that it took nearly forty dollars an hour just to keep his office open. Funding expert witnesses would also be expensive. Evidentiary items would need to be examined: weapons, casings, bullets, wood samples, and pathological reports. As a bottom line, the resourceful defense counsel requested that ten thousand dollars be placed in trust for experts and paralegal work, and attorney fees upped to seventy dollars an hour to compensate the anticipated loss from private clients paying higher fees.

"Could we discuss my motion in chambers?" Sloan asked. The judge granted his request.

As attorneys exited the courtroom, Elmer and Patrick grew suspicious that something was up. "Are we being sold out again?" Elmer asked Patrick.

While in chambers, Sloan repeated his laundry list of funding requests, but his tone turned negative midway into the discussion. Without warning, he looked at his file and addressed the judge. "After considerable thought, I think I best withdraw as Mr. Hoffman's attorney."

Sloan explained, "I received a call from Gary Bray, a witness who might be subpoenaed to testify. Bray expressed fears that he might be a suspect in the incident involving Hoffman and McGinnis." Sloan pointed out that Bray had made the call from Washington State Corrections Center at Shelton.

"I'd like to stay on the case, but I don't want to get written up in the state bar news publication over a conflict of interest issue," Sloan said. Judge Alumbaugh was prepared to grant his motion for increased fees, but as she later noted, "The more Sloan argued for the fees, at some point he convinced himself he best withdraw."

The attorneys and judge returned to the courtroom. "I request that I withdraw as Patrick Hoffman's attorney," Sloan said.

"Your request is granted," replied the judge, turning her attention to the defendants. "The court will now hear arguments as to how we proceed. Should today's motions be rescheduled to find a substitute attorney for Mr. Hoffman?"

Deputy Prosecutor Jack Burchard, recently elected as the new county prosecutor, stood at his table. "I object to postponing motions scheduled for today's hearing. There are two issues that require timely rulings: the state's motion to evaluate Elmer McGinnis's competency to stand trial, and removal of a bullet lodged in defendant McGinnis's arm. The bullet is crucial to this case," the prosecutor argued. "These motions are entirely personal and restricted to Elmer McGinnis. Hearing these matters would have no adverse effect on Patrick Hoffman."

Although Bud Gardner represented Elmer McGinnis, Gardner in Sloan's absence argued, "Patrick Hoffman requires an attorney. The bullet lodged in Elmer's arm could have implications as to the guilt or innocence of Patrick Hoffman."

Burchard disputed the claim. "Removal of the bullet and identification of the weapon firing the round deal with defendant McGinnis's argument of self-defense and have no adverse effect on Patrick Hoffman's defense."

The judge looked at Elmer and ruled, "We will proceed today only with the two motions: one for a competency assessment and the other to have a bullet removed from defendant McGinnis."

Burchard formally put forth the two motions.

Patrick angrily stood and cried, "I have had problems up to this time obtaining adequate counsel. It's becoming a farce."

"Your response is noted for the record. Please proceed with the motion for a competency assessment of Mr. McGinnis," the judge said.

Burchard began, "The petition—"

"I know my rights," Patrick interrupted. "I have a right to have a lawyer."

"Your objection is noted for the record," the judge repeated.

Later, the judge wrote in her notes that she feared the muscular defendant was at a point of losing control. Patrick sat down with his eyes still fixated on the judge.

Elmer would not be still over these developments. He yelled, "This is bullshit." Gardner did his best to quell him again, but to no avail. "Bullshit, bullshit," Elmer muttered. The disruptions were making it difficult for the court reporter or judge to hear attorneys. Elmer pushed closer and closer to expulsion from the hearing. "Goddamnit, where can you get any justice? This is pure bullshit. All this only to muzzle me about corruption," Elmer shouted. He pointed his finger at the judge. "The charges have been dismissed, and you know damn well that's the case."

"Mr. McGinnis, you are out of order. Restrain yourself, or you will be removed from the court."

Bud Gardner answered for Elmer. "My client is only expressing his concern for a fair hearing."

The judge acknowledged Mr. Gardner's remark and requested that the prosecutor continue.

Burchard stated, "Mr. Gardner has previously agreed to a petition to assess his client's competency. My motion is to refer Elmer McGinnis to Eastern State Hospital and determine his competency to stand trial."

Elmer exploded. "Bullshit! Pure bullshit! This is only for one reason—sending me to a loony bin to shut me up."

Again, Bud Gardner came to his feet, shouting over Elmer, "The court needs to understand my client is only expressing his legitimate point of view. He believes certain members of the Colville Reservation want to shut him up."

Patrick stood tall and shouted, "I protest in the strongest way. How you rule on Dad being crazy affects me."

"Again, your objection is noted for the record. Please proceed, Mr. Burchard," replied the judge.

"Elmer McGinnis has fired attorneys, shouted obscenities in court, and made rambling statements in a recent television interview," Burchard said. "We have preliminary evidence from mental health providers who evaluated Mr. McGinnis that he has serious mental issues." Burchard looked up at the judge. "It is clear from the defendant's belligerent behavior in court that there is a question about whether he can assist in his own defense or understand the proceedings, including communication with his attorney."

Mr. Gardner rose. "While I understand my client's concerns, the major question before the court is not his competency but whether my client can assist in his defense. My client is competent."

Gardner was in a bind. If Elmer was competent, a self-defense argument was a likely option. If his client had mental issues, a mitigation argument was in order. Since he had only a few weeks to interview his client, there was no way to resolve with any certainty which option was best. The first order of business was to see what experts might conclude as to his client's mental status. To that end, Gardner reserved any reactions to Burchard's motion.

The judge announced, "Mr. McGinnis, you will be sent to Eastern State Hospital to determine your competency to stand trial."

Elmer McGinnis again raged, "Bullshit! Total and complete bullshit." His voice quavered, and his hands exhibited a noticeable palsy.

Ignoring Elmer's outburst, Burchard continued. "We request that the court give authority to medical experts to remove a bullet lodged in Elmer McGinnis. This could be critical forensic evidence in this case; experts could possibly determine what gun delivered the nearly fatal shot to Elmer McGinnis."

Perhaps anticipating that the bullet might show that an officer other than John Dick or Louis Millard shot Elmer McGinnis, Gardner agreed to the motion. Judge Alumbaugh ordered the removal of the bullet from defendant McGinnis if the procedure could be done safely. She set the next hearing for December 19. Fees were set aside for the defense to solicit their own psychiatric expert and hire a criminologist and legal assistant. After other housekeeping details were resolved, the stormy first day of pretrial was gaveled to an end.

Chapter 13

Pretrial Skirmishes

December 19, 1986

The early morning pretrial hearings dealt with defense motions regarding the lack of access to physical evidence and motions for continuance. Richard Price, a local attorney, accepted the court's request that he serve as Patrick Hoffman's attorney. Price was atop the list of available attorneys to take the assignment. However, Price worried that the case would crowd out his active civil practice. In spite of these reservations, the busy attorney agreed to represent Patrick.

Court was brought to order. "Your Honor, I must express with a high degree of urgency that the state make available crucial evidence that could exonerate Mr. Hoffman," the newly appointed counsel said. Price outlined in meticulous detail the lack of cooperation on the part of prosecutors to obtain guns, bullets, clothing, wood portions allegedly penetrated by bullets, and all other physical items removed from or near the McGinnis property. "The defense is in an untenable position of completing a forensic examination of the physical evidence with only ten days left until the trial begins," Price argued.

"The defendants and their attorneys caused much of their predicament," Burchard rebutted. "They knew full well of the sixty-day rule.

To date, the defendants have had four attorneys. During that time, none have interviewed or attempted to interview any of the witnesses listed by the state."

As for the delay of the competency examination of Elmer McGinnis, Burchard cited a previous conversation with Owen Gardner. "Mr. Gardner told me he believed his client should undergo a competency examination, but his client would not allow him to apply for one. The delay occurred because of the defendant's resistance and the turnover of judges to hear the motion." With regard to the physical evidence held by the FBI, Burchard argued, "Our office has made several calls to the FBI agents responsible for the lab work, attempting to expedite their report and return of the physical evidence."

Judge Alumbaugh was not persuaded. "Lab evidence is critical to the defense. I see this as a problem with the source," she said. "Evidence is to be delivered to Ray Davis, defense forensic expert in Seattle, no later than December twenty-fourth."

December 24, 1986

For the pretrial hearing on Christmas Eve, no carols of peace on earth were heard, or at least, not recorded in the trial transcript. The FBI had not returned the physical evidence. Court matters dealt with whether statements made by the defendants after their arrest were admissible.

Officers who found Elmer on the hillside were called to recount the statements Elmer made while in critical condition. Deputy Murray cited how he had read Elmer his rights, and Elmer had indicated he understood his rights. Deputy Mayo repeated his statement to FBI Agent Davis; he quoted Elmer as saying he shot at a light that was directed at him.

The day ended with attorneys jockeying on the prosecutor's motion that the trial date be extended five days beyond the December 29 startup date. Burchard pled that many more witnesses were scheduled for pretrial and could not be heard in that short time. The motion was affirmed. To speed up matters, the judge suggested scheduling a hearing after Christmas on the twenty-sixth.

Defense attorneys objected that this was insufficient time to prepare for their pending motions.

Price further argued, "I don't see anything in the record here about due diligence in terms of the manpower that they've employed." Price was referring to the three prosecutors on the case: Boole, Burchard, and Hicks. Boole would remain on the case until his term ended January 1987. The outgoing prosecutor had also appointed Earl Hicks as a state deputy prosecutor.

Price went on. "The state was certainly aware of the crimes charged and the requirements of the sixty-day rule. They have not facilitated in any way the availability of the evidence to the defense."

Judge Alumbaugh said, "There has been due diligence from all attorneys to respond to the court's requests, get these matters set, and get it heard as soon as possible. Delay has been caused in part by disqualifications of previous judges: two by the defendants and one by the state. I am concerned that the pretrial hearings be conducted in an orderly fashion so the court can give these motions due weight and avoid an intemperate decision based on trial date."

December 29, 1986

The court scheduled hearings on December 29 and 30 out of necessity. Each hearing dealt with motions on suppression of evidence regarding Elmer McGinnis's remarks to officers when they found him on the hillside. Also, motions for a continuance of the trial date were offered. The defense submitted yet another motion that discovery was not being provided. The FBI still had not delivered all evidentiary items to the defense.

On the matter of Elmer McGinnis's hillside "death confessions," mental health experts testified that none of the factors regarding his medical condition, including his mental status, affected any knowing and intelligent waiver of his rights.

Judge Alumbaugh ruled that McGinnis's statements were voluntary. Later in the hearing, Bud Gardner asserted, "My client will not rely on insanity or incompetence to stand trial as a defense." Elmer had insisted that his attorney drop the crazy alibi, saying, "We are innocent. Why are these shrinks involved in the first place?"

Price was frustrated that most of the pretrial motions dealt with Elmer McGinnis—his alleged statements and mental status. In a brief to the court, Price argued that Hoffman had not confronted the Colville Business Council and was not the target for arrest when police invaded the McGinnis property. Patrick was forced to defend his father and himself during the shooting incident.

"How can defendant Hoffman mount a defense without access to the items I have previously requested?" Price asked. "Furthermore, why have portions of the federal grand jury records been redacted? Why have we not received a full record providing the questions asked by grand jurors? Is there something the state is hiding?"

"Nothing is being hidden," replied Burchard. "The redacted portions are to protect the identity of the jurors."

"There is no way to validate that claim other than an examination of the complete record," Price replied. "I request we be given the full record."

"Your request is denied. Grand jury privacy will be maintained. The court will conduct an in-camera review to ascertain what redacted portions are possible evidence for the defense," the judge said.

The defense hoped the redacted material might expose police misconduct or damning exculpatory evidence of their engagement in the firefight, but results were disappointing. Judge Alumbaugh concluded, "None of the evidence I reviewed in the grand jury proceedings spoke to the defendants' guilt or innocence. Most of the deleted commentary concerned jurors' questions about matters of law pertaining to the federal charges before the grand jury."

December 30, 1986

Significant motions—one questioning the jurisdiction of the state court and another requesting that the defendants be tried separately—had not been heard. A jury had not been selected.

The trial date had to be resolved. The defense faced a dilemma. Without all forensic evidence from the FBI, defense attorneys were handicapped. Was it a reasonable argument that police first fired at the coop, hitting the two officers and Elmer McGinnis? The answer required forensic examination of the two removed bullets: one from Sergeant Millard, the other from Elmer McGinnis. Raymond Davis, forensic expert for the defense, had yet to receive the bullets recovered from the victims.

Burchard conditionally favored a continuance if the defense agreed to waive the sixty-day rule. Richard Price and Bud Gardner had mixed views. Gardner felt it was important to conduct further investigations of witnesses and to speed up the FBI's delivery of physical evidence to Ray Davis, who needed sufficient time to complete his own assessment. Price accused prosecutors and FBI lab experts of dragging their collective heels to avoid exposure of embarrassing inconsistencies in their theory of the case. While Gardner agreed with Price in principle, he felt it was impossible to meet the court's January 5 deadline.

"Yes, a lengthy continuance is needed," conceded Price. "However, my client is charged with premeditated murder. The majority of testimony so far has primarily involved Hoffman's father and tribal police. There is no incontrovertible evidence that my client has killed or wounded anyone." Price emphasized that the rationale for the state supreme court's sixty-day rule was to provide the highest degree of protection for this type of case. "I'm in a box, but it's not a box of my making. It's a catch twenty-two depending upon how this court deals with it and maybe how some higher tribunals look at it. I think the court would be remiss at this point if it found that Mr. Hoffman was prepared to go to trial. The state has manipulated the sixty-day rule by withholding evidence, knowing that the defense was in no position to proceed."

Burchard took exception. "A number of documents have already been provided to the defendants."

"The problem is not providing a paper trail of evidence as it is available," Gardner said. "The real difficulty is sorting through the mountains of documents and the retarded arrival of physical evidence to our experts."

Judge Alumbaugh realized the matter of a continuance had to be resolved. Court error could happen either way she ruled: to enforce or not enforce the sixty-day rule. Defendants really held the trump cards based on previous case law. The state supreme court had granted few exceptions to prosecutors requesting an extension of the sixty-day rule.

The judge asked attorneys to chambers. Discussion of a possible trial date generated much disagreement. Attorneys repeated their arguments as to why motions had not been heard and possible remedies. Finally the judge halted debate and made a call. "A continuance will be granted to the defendants if both waive their right to a speedy trial. Otherwise, the court is ready to proceed to trial starting on the fifth of January." The defense attorneys huddled and ultimately reached an accord. The judge requested that all parties return to the courtroom.

"I understand an agreement has been reached. A continuance will extend the trial date beyond the fifth of January, given the right to a speedy trial is waived," the judge offered.

With no objections, Judge Alumbaugh set the trial to begin February 17. An extensive backlog of preliminary matters awaited hearing. Forensic investigations were incomplete; jury instructions had yet to be specified; the onerous issues of jurisdiction and whether the defendants would be tried together were unresolved. Added to that list, there remained the task of jury selection.

Chapter 14

Trial Delay

Pretrial hearings extended into January and most of February 1987. Motions required more time than anticipated to adjudicate. As February 17 approached, it was clear that the trial would have to be set back again. The judge agreed to reschedule the trial for February 26.

All forensic evidence was not delivered to the defense by January 17 as promised. The judge showed little patience. "All materials are to be delivered to the defense by January 30, no exceptions." For unknown reasons, the FBI failed to comply. At a February 10 pretrial hearing, Burchard notified the court that the FBI evidence had finally been delivered to the defense forensic expert, Ray Davis.

During the hearing, Elmer complained to Gardner about the pace of the trial. "When are you going to get to the corruption? Why is it taking so damn long?" A jury still had not been selected. Arguments over the legality of search warrants on the McGinnis property were lengthy. Gardner challenged whether individuals had properly searched Elmer's truck or the Impala, which had been impounded by police.

Another defense motion requiring most of a trial day dealt with alleged domestic problems John Dick had experienced a decade ago. A source for the defense reported that Dick had been involved in a domestic dispute with his wife and had threatened to take his own life. In the motion, Richard Price called for an examination of Dick's police personnel record for the last ten years. In addition, he asked that Dick be assessed by a psychiatrist to evaluate potential violent tendencies.

Burchard argued that Dick's privacy was at issue given that he was currently undergoing treatment at Fairfax Hospital to deal with the traumatic loss of his partner.

"The motion requiring a mental health assessment is denied," the judge determined. "Privacy rights come into play while John Dick is being treated."

Price countered, "The defense is entitled to search for a pattern of violence that could affect events on the morning of the shooting incident. There could be a pattern of violence in John Dick's history to explain actions that may have precipitated the shooting. Such a search should include access to his personnel file."

"I will not grant defense access to his file until the court has had an opportunity to review it in its entirety," announced the judge. "Mr. Dick's personnel records are protected." After reading the personnel file delivered by tribal police, the judge ruled, "I could find no incident in John Dick's personnel file that speaks to the question of assaultive or gratuitous violence. Access is denied."

The pretrial was slowed in part by the method used to transcribe the proceedings. The Okanogan court reporter, Peggy Melvin, spoke quietly into a large cone-shaped voice-recording device, and later transcribed the recording. The older courtroom amplified ambient noise, making it difficult for Melvin to simultaneously hear and make an accurate record. She requested repeats, particularly when speech was rapid or the witness did not speak up. In addition, the mere volume of trial records proved overwhelming, making for slow turnaround of transcripts.

Judge Alumbaugh asked Melvin if she would like relief, and Melvin welcomed the offer. Kittitas County court reporter Jewel Smith agreed to assist Melvin with her heavy workload. It worked. The backlog of transcripts was reduced, and disputes over previous testimony faded.

The judge scheduled jury selection for February 17, and notices were sent out to Okanogan residents.

February 17, 1986

Tedious debates erupted over how the court should proceed to strike an unbiased jury. Judge Alumbaugh reminded attorneys that the number of peremptory challenges had to be resolved sooner than later. These challenges, legal in Washington courts, allowed attorneys to strike a juror from selection without citing cause. F. Lee Bailey, one of OJ Simpson's dream team of lawyers, once commented that most trials are won or lost by jury selection.

For most jury panels, it goes without saying that each side would want to maximize the number of challenges to strike a panel least biased against their client or theory of the case. Attorneys generally rely on their experience and intuition to make challenges.

Not too surprisingly, the defense was quite displeased with Judge Alumbaugh's initial proposal on jury selection. The judge proposed the defense be allowed eight peremptory challenges and the prosecution six. Given the heavy press coverage, both defense attorneys felt more challenges would be necessary to find an impartial jury.

Attorneys argued for a day and a half over the number of peremptory challenges. The judge finally brought closure. "The number of challenges is not a constitutional right, only the right to question jurors for bias and prejudice in judging the facts of the case," she reminded attorneys. "Given the heavy press coverage and difficulties of finding unbiased panelists, I have concluded that both sides be given leeway. Without objection, the defense will be allowed twelve challenges, and the state allowed eight challenges."

Given the number of challenges provided to each side, jury selection was painfully slow. From the defense's perspective, how many unbiased or untainted panelists could be found, given the one-sided news accounts available?

As to selecting Colville enrollees for the jury panel, prosecutors legally were restricted from striking panelists based on their ethnicity. However, that did not necessarily mean that Colville enrollees would be found in large numbers in the original jury pool. Jury pools consisted of registered voters who possessed a valid driver's license. Accordingly, there was no way to determine the number of Colville enrollees screened disproportionately due to not having a valid driver's license and voting record.

On the first day, only two panelists were selected. If only the defense would agree to the ten-minute rule the judge had set forth, Burchard complained, "two days should have been more than enough to pick this jury. At this pace we're going, it's going to take a long time just to get through the first twelve. On top of that, we have to pick two alternates."

"I suppose all of us feel time pressures, but we're trying to be as careful as possible," replied the judge. "Striking a panel that minimizes potential bias is more important than moving hastily to an expedited trial date."

Somewhat dramatically during the colloquy over jury selection, Richard Price introduced a motion to dismiss the panel proceedings. He held up a front-page article from the February 18, 1987, home edition of the *Wenatchee World*. He read the headline, "Father and Son Go on Trial for Murder," and then pointed out egregious errors in reporting. For example, "Dick survived because a bulletproof vest deflected two rifle bullets."

Price wanted to throw out all the selected jurors and start another trial. His strongly worded plea asserted that the *Wenatchee World* article contained so many inflammatory and highly prejudiced representations of the defendants that striking an unbiased jury would be very difficult if not impossible.

"I am not exasperated; I'm mad," Price proclaimed. "Everyone on the venire panel needs to be asked whether they saw the pictures or the article or discussed the article with anyone else." The article talked about McGinnis and Hoffman ambushing police officers when they tried to arrest McGinnis at his Nespelem home. "Some of McGinnis's neighbors on the Colville Indian Reservation say the World War II sharpshooter was a perverse old man, and was willing to argue about anything."

Price quoted from the paper, "'Defense attorneys would try to prove a bullet from a police rifle killed Millard.' If such a defense was in the offing, it's news to me." The article contained other misstatements regarding how Officer Millard was killed, how Officer Dick survived because of the deflection of two rifle bullets, and how Officer Clark was shot in the thumb, which later turned out to be false.

Price argued, "These distortions are potentially so biasing that a gag order is required against the press, specifically the *Wenatchee World*." Bud Gardner agreed. "News accounts going back to August 1986 after the shootings have made references to 'massacre attack' and 'ambush' to describe the defendants' stand against police."

Even Burchard agreed with defense attorneys. "I was disturbed by the article, as was Mr. Hicks, and I don't know what to do about it. But as for a gag motion, the media frequently gets a story wrong, and readers come to expect stories are not always based on valid facts. The remedy for selecting jurors is to ask each if they were aware of the article; and for those exposed to the pictures, headlines, or story details, what conclusions had they had drawn, if any?" he said. "Such media distortions are not unusual. There is no need to be hysterical about this."

The defense argued that other papers had published similar accounts. Then, Price upped the ante. "At a minimum, this court should dismiss the entire venire panel, or better yet change the venue. Trying the defendants in a different jurisdiction is the fairest way to deal with the contaminating effects of these outrageous reports." Price reinforced his claim by pointing out that the *Wenatchee World* was the major news source for Okanogan County. "Yet as biased as this paper is in their coverage, other news accounts have not shown any more balance in reporting the shootings. I don't think you can unring the bell here."

Gardner agreed. "In the small towns in and around Okanogan, people are talking about the trial. Even if an unbiased panel could be found, how could one expect jurists to follow the court's instructions to not discuss the case with anyone when media puts so much information out there?" Such articles, he went on, have enticed citizens to look for answers from news sources. "Reporters are thought to have directly examined the evidence against the defendants. People in small towns congregate frequently and chat about local affairs, whether it's at the grocery store or the coffee shop," he said. "The pressure on jurists would be extreme, especially when they realize they are part of the growing news story that everyone is talking about."

The judge had anticipated the defense would make a change of venue motion, but not this soon. "First of all, people considered for jury duty need a chance to respond truthfully to questions," she said. "If their responses show a biasing influence of media coverage so great that we can't get a jury, then we'll consider whether or not we need to change venue on this trial."

Price asked the judge when a ruling might be made on the venue question; she answered that attorneys were to go forward first, and strike a jury if possible. "We won't know until we do that whether media bias was present," she said. "We'll consider a change of venue motion if striking a jury becomes a serious problem."

Jury selection took six days, starting early in the morning and ending late afternoon. The attorneys' queries wandered and were repetitive. The judge wrote in her notes, "It is a slower process than expected to find a panelist untainted by news coverage and having no apparent conflict of interest with tribal officials or local law enforcement." Despite Burchard's early prediction that a jury could be struck in two days, neither side was about to let the other side have a favorable panel. Each panelist was carefully scrutinized for any hint of prejudice toward their version of events.

Fourteen panelists were selected, two as alternates. Four jurists listed reservation addresses, three from Nespelem and one from Elmer City. The remainder listed their addresses off the Colville Reservation, spreading north to Tonasket, Twisp, and Oroville, and south to Omak, Okanogan, and Grand Coulee. There were nine male jurists; the remaining five jurists were women.

There was no way to determine the precise number of Colville enrollees or other Native Americans, if any, selected from the original jury pool. Elmer McGinnis likely knew some of the panelists. He bitterly complained that not a single Colville was selected.

Chapter 15

Contentious Beginning

On the cold and overcast day of February 26, 1987, the trial finally started, some five months after the arraignment. The atmosphere was tense. The courtroom was packed with the curious and others such as family members of Louis Millard. Off-duty law enforcement officers were in attendance out of respect and concern for justice for their fellow lawman, Sergeant Louis Millard. Activists and friends of Elmer McGinnis were also there. News reporters primarily from Eastern Washington news outlets covered the trial. No cameras were allowed.

Residents were concerned that the trial had taken too long. The defense thought much of such criticism had been sparked by a *Wenatchee World* claim that trial expenses had reached six figures. As Price later argued, the underlying message to voters was clear: their taxpayer dollars were being wasted on two defendants who, according to earlier stories, had ambushed police. The narrative was that the county budget, with such a small revenue base, could hardly absorb such a hit.

The defendants sat stoically, waiting for the trial to begin. Elmer was much healthier. He had recovered from his bullet wound. He looked stronger, though he still had a noticeable tremor in his hands.

Patrick had lost some weight. During pretrial hearings, the defiant defendant had gone on a hunger strike over conditions in the county jail. However, there were no ill effects. His physical fitness and handsome facial features stood out.

Observers filed through a security check and attempted to find a seat in the crowded courtroom. Chatter grew louder as observers awaited the start of the trial. The bailiff came forward and waited for the din of the crowd to grow silent. "All rise. The Okanogan County Superior Court is now in session. The Honorable Judge Jo Anne Alumbaugh is presiding." The judge stepped up to the bench and seated herself confidently in the oversized chair. "Please be seated," announced the bailiff.

"Good Morning, ladies and gentlemen," the judge said. "I am calling the case of the State of Washington versus Elmer McGinnis and Patrick Hoffman. Are both parties ready to go forward?"

"Yes, Your Honor," both parties announced.

Elmer and Patrick listened respectfully. Their demeanor and dress contrasted radically with their appearance on the first day of the pretrial. Their surliness was gone. Elmer's restlessness had abated. Patrick had found a jacket, and Elmer a nice shirt and pants. Their appearance stood in stark contrast to their unkempt jail fatigues of three months ago.

The judge moved to matters at hand. "Is the state prepared to make its opening statement?"

By precedent, prosecutors have the first and last word in making a case against defendants. Since English Common Law centuries ago, jurists have reasoned that, since the trier of fact must prove that the accused are guilty beyond reasonable doubt, prosecutors should be afforded this advantage.

As Burchard approached the jury to make his opening statement, Patrick made a point to fixate his eyes on Burchard's. Burchard likely was unaware of Patrick's glare, or if he was, he looked the other way. Making eye contact with the jury was uppermost in his mind—it was important to set the right tone for the jury to follow his version of what happened.

"I can't believe how nervous I am this morning," Burchard confessed to the jury as he looked at his notes. Like the judge, his performance on this high-profile case could define his career. It was a matter of developing momentum, as he did while serving as a defense attorney. Among attorneys, Burchard was known as an excellent litigator, winning virtually all his cases.

The prosecutor caught his breath, put down his notes, and looked at jurors one by one. "You have the task to judge whether the defendants are guilty of aggravated first-degree murder and aggravated assault. I think of the jury's decision sort of like the picture on the box of one of these picture puzzles— jigsaw puzzles. Some people like to work them without looking at the picture. I like to look at the picture," he said.

"If you take a bird's-eye view like the picture puzzle, your task as a juror is to determine whether the defendants Elmer McGinnis and Patrick Hoffman killed a person and criminally assaulted another. The person killed was a tribal police officer, Sergeant Louis Millard. The other person assaulted with deadly force was Assistant Chief John Dick." Burchard explained the elements necessary to convict the accused of aggravated first-degree murder and aggravated first-degree assault. He explained what "intent" meant for a first-degree murder charge and how "aggravation" referred in this trial to assault on police officers carrying out their duty.

The prosecutor then began his account of what happened, starting with the attempt to arrest Elmer McGinnis at the Tribal Council office and ending with Patrick Hoffman's comments made to Jeff Epperson and Fred Leskinen. He described Elmer's scuffle with police at the Tribal Council office, his subsequent treatment for a heart condition at an Omak hospital, how he left the hospital unauthorized with his children, and how police identified Lila McGinnis's car and followed in pursuit.

Burchard described how Elmer and his family took off onto logging roads and parked. "Elmer told his daughters, 'I don't want you girls to be in the line of fire.' Inside the trunk of the car, Patrick Hoffman had a gym bag containing three loaded weapons," the prosecutor emphasized. "Five hours later, Elmer and his son had made their way to Nespelem and ultimately the

McGinnis home. In the meantime, police continued searching for Mr. McGinnis and Mr. Hoffman without any success.

"Officer Brian Phillips, who was ordered to conduct surveillance on the McGinnis house, saw two figures approaching the house about one thirty in the morning. Officer Phillips called in on his radio to his commanding officer, Lou Millard, for orders. Sergeant Millard instructed him to intercept them. Brian Phillips indicated it was too dark to see where they were. Lou Millard, who was driving back to his home in Keller, turned his car around and headed for the McGinnis home."

The prosecutor then referred to a diagram showing the location of the McGinnis house, the street toward the north, Cache Creek Road, the barbed-wire fence surrounding the McGinnis property, and the sloped pasture to the south leading to a forested area. To the east, he pointed out an access road parallel to the McGinnis property.

"After Phillips's report, Chief John Dick and Lou Millard made the decision to search an old house to the east near the McGinnis property and found nothing," the prosecutor proclaimed. "Both officers continued toward the McGinnis property, climbed over the barbed-wire fence marking the boundary, and proceeded toward the back of the McGinnis property. Both had their police-issued flashlights turned on, searching for the two men. As they conversed about having to lose some weight because of the tough time getting over the fence, they heard a noise to the south. They shined their flashlights back toward the pasture area behind the McGinnis property and spotted a horse."

"Dick then walked toward a chicken coop in the backyard of the McGinnis property. His flashlight was directed toward the backside of the building, and he saw no doors. Dick then turned around, walking back toward Sergeant Millard. After the initial step or two, he was shot in the back by one of the two defendants. The bullet entered his left shoulder and exited through his chest, knocking him to the ground. Dick called out to Millard that he had been hit.

"Sergeant Millard drew his service revolver and got off two shots before he was hit. The bullet entered his chest immediately below his neck, above the bulletproof vest he was wearing at the time. Dick could hear Millard moaning, but he couldn't find him in the dark.

"The defendants then fired flares to light up the area. Dick could now see Millard and could hear gurgling sounds from the downed officer. His fellow officer could not talk. Dick grabbed Millard's belt and tried to drag him to cover behind a cement barrier. As Dick crawled toward protection, trying to drag Millard to safety, the downed officers were continuously under attack. More flares were shot, setting the area on fire as bullets were directed at the officers. Dick was able to draw his weapon and fire five shots at the muzzle flashes from guns directed at him and his partner. One of his shots hit Elmer McGinnis in the middle of his chest," the prosecutor said. "The bullet was later removed from Mr. McGinnis, and forensic analysis indicates that the bullet most likely was shot from John Dick's .357 revolver.

"Patrick Hoffman and Elmer McGinnis had three guns. They fired eighteen shots at the officers and fired two flare guns with at least seven flares to illuminate their targets. Officers Millard and Dick fired their weapons, a total of seven shots. No other officer fired their weapon.

"After the shooting ceased, two Okanogan deputies were sent up the hill to search a wooded area about two hundred yards south of the house. An officer spotted a man lying prone with what turned out to be a flare gun in his belt; he could see that the man had been shot. The officer asked if he was the owner of the property, and the man identified himself as Elmer McGinnis. The officer read his rights before taking a statement. Elmer said he had been ambushed. He said he saw a flashlight and instinctively shot at it.

"Elmer was treated for his gunshot wound and transferred to the Spokane County Jail. The evidence will show that Patrick Hoffman abandoned his father on the hillside and took off toward Keller. He took with him a 9-millimeter semiautomatic assault weapon, what some label a machine pistol, specifically, an Interdynamics Tech Mini 9."

Richard Price immediately rose from counsel's table. "I object to the prosecutor introducing evidence that has not yet been established."

"Your objection is sustained," the judge replied. "Mr. Burchard, you must limit your remarks to what the evidence will show, not what it is."

"Evidence will be introduced to describe this 9-millimeter gun," Burchard said. "Pat Hoffman disposed of the weapon on his way to Keller." With slowness and deference, the prosecutor said, "This is the gun that was used to kill the officer. The bullet recovered from Lou Millard's body was a 9-millimeter, fully jacketed bullet. Further, two empty cartridges found at the scene were 9-millimeter pieces of brass."

Burchard continued, describing Patrick's nearly two-day trip, leaving his father and heading for the Epperson place in Keller. "When Jeffrey told Patrick that Lou Millard was dead, Patrick said as he looked him in the eye, 'Good Deal. Good Deal.'

"Hoffman asked Jeff Epperson and Fred Leskinen to help him get away. Both Jeff and Fred talked him in to turning himself in to Okanogan County Sheriff Johnston." The prosecutor described how the threesome made their way to Sheriff Johnston's office. "On the way, Hoffman told them he had used the 9-millimeter gun and had gotten rid of it while traversing mountainous terrain between Nespelem and Keller. Patrick's friends heard him say, 'I fired a weapon or weapons but I didn't shoot at anyone.' Patrick also told them that he had used a nine-millimeter gun."

The prosecutor ended his opening. "The evidence will show beyond reasonable doubt that the defendants by means and intent carried out a deadly assault on tribal police officers, resulting in the death of Louis Millard and wounding of John Dick."

Chapter 16

Defense Rebuttal

Gardner and Price had argued repeatedly that each defendant should be tried separately. Throughout the trial, Price strongly argued that Patrick's motives or intent during the shooting had little or nothing to do with Elmer McGinnis's conflicts with the Colville Business Council members. After a lengthy pretrial debate, the judge was not persuaded.

In a nutshell, the judge saw the two defenses fundamentally as one of self-defense. Washington Appellate and Supreme Court decisions favored trying defendants together when jointly accused of committing criminal acts. An exception was when the state offered the testimony of one defendant against the other. In this instance, Jeffrey Epperson testified during pretrial that Patrick told him Elmer had fired the 9-millimeter during the shoot-out. The judge ruled that Mr. Epperson's testimony regarding Mr. McGinnis's alleged actions would not be allowed.

Given the judge's denial of the severance motion, Price realized he had to make a strong first impression to separate Patrick's perspective in the jury's view. Elmer's difficulties with the council agency and tribal police were not in any way linked to Patrick. The escalation of events that led to a combative arrest and police intrusion on the McGinnis property, which led to the shooting incident, were all about Elmer McGinnis.

Richard Price rose, and with a steady and convincing stride toward the jury, he visually addressed each juror as he spoke. "This case is really about how each individual understood what was happening on the morning of August twenty-seventh. Take the example of an automobile accident where five people who witness the incident give five different accounts of what happened. Those people are not lying; it's because they've come at it from different backgrounds, different perceptions, and they have different abilities.

"It was a set of events beyond the defendants' control that led to a tragic event. Observers of this event, like in the automobile example, have offered different stories of what happened. If you view this as a tragic event rather than criminal assault, you can see that tribal officers may have panicked, drawn their weapons, and fired them just as Officers Dick and Millard had done."

Price asked jurors to look at so-called facts contextually. He pointed out that it was the confluence of events that resulted in the shooting incident. One weapon was fired, and the gun battle that never should have happened was ignited.

"Who observed what?" was the quintessential challenge to the jury. As to officers present at the incident, Price claimed their intense fear of Elmer distorted their partial accounts of what happened in those early morning hours. "Not all observers are equal. Some heard and observed these events with better acuity." In the end, he asked jurors to consider these aspects when evaluating the accuracy of witness accounts.

Price warned jurors about other words like "victim" and "defendant," which implied an innocent participant involved in an incident was harmed by the accused. The clever and neatly dressed counsel pushed this characterization throughout his opening remarks. "First, you need to look beyond the shooting incident as a starting point to determine what triggered these tragic events." Price implored the jury to see that the case began much earlier with Mr. McGinnis. "Without Mr. McGinnis, there would be no Mr. Hoffman as a defendant in this case."

Price continued his attack on the use of labels. "The facts are going to show that there were no victims as such, there were no slayers as such. Keep an open mind. That means you're going to have to say that the police officers and the defendants are all in there together, and you don't know at this point who the victims are and who the slayers are."

Price then shifted his narrative to Elmer McGinnis, describing him as a lifelong resident of the Colville Reservation who had several confrontations with neighbors and the Colville Business Council. "McGinnis's charges against the council centered on mismanagement of funds dealing with tribal lands," Price said. "Tensions grew to a point where McGinnis came to believe that there was a bounty out on his son's life—Patrick Hoffman's life.

"Initially, Patrick laughed it off, but over time, Mr. Hoffman began to wonder about the statement and became concerned about it." Price said the testimony would show that Elmer McGinnis approached Chief Smiskin in a very irate manner two and a half weeks before the shooting, and demanded to know if his police officers were involved in a conspiracy to get his son. Chief Smiskin grew concerned about the degree of rage directed at him and his officers.

"Was he a dangerous man?" Price rhetorically asked the jury. Price cited how tribal police and others in the community feared to confront him. "Mr. McGinnis was widely known to have a large arsenal in his home, and made it clear he would defend his family and himself if threatened by anyone."

Price pointed out that tribal police grew more threatened by Elmer's reputation. It was a simple incident that brought the tension to a head. McGinnis attempted to collect a debt on the sale of a motorcycle owned by his daughter, Lila McGinnis. "Upon attempting to collect payment, the party owing a payment filed a complaint against Elmer McGinnis for a misdemeanor offense, a lands-trespass charge. The complaint was a good case of one neighbor wanting to get back at the other." Price then summarized the scuffle in Dale Kohler's office, the damage to McGinnis, and the aftermath at Mid-Valley Hospital.

Price paused and pivoted to Patrick's early years of development. He described Patrick's early upbringing with his adoptive parents and how he came to know McGinnis, his natural father, and their more recent relationship.

As to how Patrick was adopted by the Hoffman family, McGinnis's wife left him with a five-month-old son, Patrick. McGinnis decided he could not raise his son properly, and contacted his neighbors and friends to see if any might rear his newborn son. Clarence and Helen Hoffman from Keller agreed to take Patrick as their son. They had a large family but felt that would not limit their care and support for the infant.

"During his teenage years, the Hoffman grandchildren teased Patrick that Clarence and Helen Hoffman were not his real parents," Price told the jury. "When Patrick confronted his parents, Clarence and Helen acknowledged that he was adopted. Patrick grew up as a Hoffman and remained loyal to them through his adulthood."

After adventuresome years outside the reservation, Patrick returned to live with the Hoffmans. He worked for the tribe as a human resource intern, assisting the elderly and doing roadwork with a private contractor. During the 1970s, he formed a rock band and played in various settings around the reservation. It was during this time that Patrick grew to know his natural father, Elmer McGinnis.

"Sometime around Thanksgiving of 1985, Patrick was convinced that McGinnis was onto something about corruption. Ultimately, Patrick came to believe there was council misconduct or mismanagement. McGinnis told his son that money was being funneled between projects to keep them open," Price said. "One example involved the Mount Tolman project: mined ore was unprofitable, yet somehow the mining continued."

Then Price shifted to his main focus. "Patrick Hoffman had no knowledge of the trespass complaint or his father's scuffle with tribal police." At the time, Patrick lived in Keller with his sister, Francis Peoples, and had never resided with McGinnis.

Price reviewed in detail the events leading to McGinnis's brawl with tribal police and hospitalization at Mid-Valley. "When they left Mid-Valley Hospital on August twenty-sixth, the lives of McGinnis and Hoffman were joined in that vehicle." Price raised his voice. "Patrick Hoffman had nothing to do with the attempted arrest or hospitalization of his father."

This statement bridged forthcoming testimony indicating that family members made no attempt to aid McGinnis's escape. The evidence was clearly absent.

Price explained that one must look at the context. "Consider that Mr. McGinnis had been beaten up at the tribal offices. He was traumatized. Medical testimony will show that he had three fractured ribs and required certain breathing devices. The altercation with police left him concerned about his family and their preservation. His intention was to avoid a confrontation with police," Price emphasized.

"When McGinnis directed his daughters to get in the car and drive off, he truly believed the tribal police would not harm them as long as he wasn't around." Price further explained why Elmer demanded to get out of the car at Armstrong Meadows. "Hoffman was forced to make a choice, which turned out not to be a non-choice. Patrick was not about to abandon his father, given his health and the late hour. Patrick felt that, one way or another, they would make their way back home."

Price described the late evening call Tribal Prosecutor Robert Widdifield made to William Cottrell, McGinnis's former attorney. "The evidence will show," Price said, "that Mr. Cottrell repeatedly asked Mr. Widdifield to call off the police pursuit to avoid a confrontation. Mr. Cottrell argued that Chief Smiskin should be persuaded to delay the search until morning. It was late, and Elmer's health was in question. Mr. Cottrell assured Mr. Widdifield that he would contact Elmer in the morning and arrange for Elmer to turn himself in. Elmer had relied strongly on Mr. Cottrell's advice over the years, and there was no reason to doubt that Mr. McGinnis would have followed his advice.

"After he exited the car, Patrick had to drag and carry McGinnis approximately seven miles to Cache Creek." Price described how the two crossed Cache Creek Road where a streetlight lit up the road and the front of the house. The pair approached the house to find the door locked. Elmer had left his keys in the ignition of the truck, the truck that was parked near the tribal agency. "The entrance to the house was on the west side. There was no front or back entrance. While on surveillance, Officer Phillips saw two men approaching the house and made a radio call. According to the officer's testimony, he couldn't identify the two individuals but thought they might be drunks."

Price then shifted his narrative to the disputed facts of the shooting incident. He emphasized that the facts would show that no police warnings were given, such as flashing colored lights, no bullhorn exhorting McGinnis to come out, or any other indication of their presence as police. "All Elmer and Patrick could see were the bright white lights shining on the property," Price explained. "The facts will show that both wanted to avoid a confrontation and be safe in their own home.

"Carden and Millard arrived after the emergency rescue vehicle was stationed on Cache Creek Road," Price said. "These two officers searched an abandoned house east of the McGinnis property. Assistant Police Chief John Dick joined them at the old house. Nothing was found."

Price explained how officers considered their options. Officer Dick opted to search an abandoned pickup. At this point, four officers, the three from the old house plus Officer Phillips, gathered around the pickup. None, said Price, had a plan or knew the precise locations each would take in the search.

"Officer Carden walked toward the front of the McGinnis house, while Officers Millard and Dick headed south along the east boundary fence line." Price walked to a diagram of the property and showed how the officers were scattered, with two headed south, one headed north and west, and the others to the north and east. "Dick, rather than going toward the house, headed southwest toward the back of the property, approaching a chicken coop."

Price said testimony would show that a bullet hit Officer Dick after he had shined his light behind the coop and turned away a step or two. "However, testimony will also show that he couldn't tell whether the shot entered his front or back when treated at the hospital. He had been knocked to the ground, and his immediate sensation was that of a bee sting in the armpit area.

"Dick righted himself and yelled," Price said. "He directed his yell… maybe at Lou Millard, or some other officer, to do something and then got down on the ground himself."

Price said there was confusion as to what was said. "Officers Phillips and Carden, positioned to the north of the property, offered different accounts of what happened. They heard somebody yell out, 'Hold it, freeze right there,' or words to that effect. Officer Phillips will testify that he thought it was Millard's voice.

"Before any shots were fired, there was a voice command: 'Stop, freeze right there,' and a retort of some sort—pardon the expression—'Fuck you,' followed immediately by the retort of a large or high-powered weapon," explained Price. "Testimony of officers other than Dick will indicate a round of rapid fire, a slight pause, and then another round of fire followed by flares going off. Sheila Cleveland, a neighbor to the north across Cache Creek Road, will testify that she could see as many as five different gun flashes in the area when the firing began.

"As the shooting broke out, Patrick was in fear for his life. He was crouched toward the west end of the chicken coop. His father was to the east. Patrick heard a shot. He turned around and he saw his father go down."

Price continued, "Patrick has weapons. Testimony will indicate that he had these weapons for a long time. He did target shooting from time to time with his friends, including Jeff Epperson. Patrick had a concealed weapon permit, and because he traveled by motorcycle, he carried his gym bag with him everywhere.

"Patrick could see that his father's wound was serious. As he held McGinnis, Patrick proceeded to defend the two of them. Flares were fired to determine who exactly was shooting at them. McGinnis had flares for his boat and kept them at home and in the back of his daughter's car. His boat was stored in Keller or Inchelium," Price said.

"The gunshots subsided. Fire broke out east of the McGinnis property due to the flares. Smoke began to roll across the area. After some time had elapsed, Patrick was quite worried that his father was dying. The younger man decided to drag his father toward the sloped area to the south, offering cover of trees." The guns were abandoned or lost as Patrick struggled to get his father over a barbed-wire fence and back under a tree. "Police later found two hand-guns in the area, .22 and .45 calibers. Regarding the alleged murder weapon, a 9-millimeter weapon was not ditched or concealed but lost in the same fashion as the .45, as Patrick tried to help his father get up into the tree area.

"While the evidence will show that a nine-millimeter bullet killed Lou Millard, a 9-millimeter weapon was not conclusively linked to the bullet. FBI reports will indicate two different versions of bullets retrieved from the crime scene. The first version was a bullet found in the field, initially thought to be a .357, .358, or 9-millimeter bullet. The second report indicates that this bullet from the field was different from the nine-millimeter bullet taken from Lou Millard." Price challenged the jury, "No evidence will show that any weapon fired by Patrick Hoffman or Elmer McGinnis entered the body of Mr. Millard."

Price ended his opening statement by reminding the jury, "Your open minds are essential. Much testimony will be confusing because of the dark-ness and the presence of others in the area, such as a Mr. Gary Bray, an indi-vidual on probation, whom witnesses saw running across the street with a gun during the shooting. We believe the testimony you are about to hear in detail, the ramifications of which I haven't begun to cover, will establish that this is not a case beyond reasonable doubt."

Chapter 17

Motion for Mistrial

The state opened their case by calling Okanogan County Sheriff Johnny Johnston to testify as to the authority of officers to enforce laws on and off the reservation. Johnston gave a detailed account of how tribal officers deputized in Okanogan County were authorized to make an arrest. The officers in question, including John Dick, Louis Millard, and Gary Carden, were authorized to make an arrest at Mid-Valley Hospital and at the McGinnis residence.

Burchard asked the sheriff, "In Millard and Dick's duties as county deputies, would they have had authority to arrest someone using a warrant issued by the Ferry County District Court?"

"Yes, they would have such authority," replied Sheriff Johnston.

Price bounded from his chair and objected. "No foundation has been established."

Answering the challenge before the ruling on the objection, Burchard stated, "I have not offered it yet, but I will make it an exhibit."

Gardner stood up and joined Mr. Price. "I strongly object also."

"Your objections are sustained," declared the judge.

The prosecutor withdrew a copy of the arrest warrant and asked, "Do you know whether or not there was an arrest warrant in existence for Patrick Hoffman on August 26 and 27, 1986, issued by the Ferry County District Court?"

Sheriff Johnston answered, "It's my understanding that there was."

Price approached the bench and insisted his objection be discussed outside the presence of the jury. His request was granted around 3:00 p.m. The jury was in for a long wait.

Price complained to the judge, "Sheriff Johnston's answer in the affirmative regarding the Ferry County arrest warrant had no purpose other than to prejudice the jury and insinuate there was a legal basis for police to be on the property. There was no evidence that any of the officers had any knowledge of the Ferry warrant on the days in question. It just—it's incredible, and I don't know how you're going to unring the bell."

The prosecutor explained, "Your Honor, our position is there's no bell whatsoever to unring. The defense has no idea what the officers were thinking since they have never talked to them. Chief Smiskin called the Ferry County Sheriff's Department and was directed to execute that warrant for Patrick Hoffman, and we will offer proof of that."

"Such a development comes as a real shock to defendant Hoffman, Your Honor," Price said. "All charges must be dismissed for lack of foundation in establishing an arrest warrant out for Patrick Hoffman. No foundation was established that Sheriff Johnston or his deputized officers were attempting to execute such a warrant on the evening of the twenty-sixth and early morning hours of the twenty-seventh. None of this was raised in pretrial. I can't imagine why this has been introduced in this fashion, but the jury has been tainted in a way that cannot be undone, and I ask for dismissal of this case."

"I was basically establishing the legal authority of the police arrest," Burchard replied. "In redirect, I asked whether they would have authority to arrest for resisting arrest, assault of a police officer, or escape, and whether they could arrest on a Ferry County District Court warrant. I was only attempting to establish that these officers had the authority to pursue an arrest."

"All charges against the defendants must be dismissed," Price demanded. "The jury has been tainted with an improper reference to an arrest warrant for Patrick Hoffman."

Judge Alumbaugh requested a recess to review the matter. Before the judge exited, Burchard explained, "Your Honor, I believe that we started arguing without you being aware of the facts. The defense was provided a copy of the arrest warrant for Mr. Hoffman, but it had not been brought to the attention of the court."

Judge Alumbaugh left the bench and returned some forty minutes later. Her displeasure was apparent. "I have no idea what the state thought it was doing, or where it was going with the proposed exhibit of an arrest warrant for a misdemeanor purportedly against Mr. Hoffman," she said loudly. "That action was incredibly inappropriate. The court is going to cure the error with an instruction at this time, but such errors have a cumulative effect." Her last statement was a warning that she would entertain a mistrial motion if any other evidence was improperly introduced.

"I admit that I could have asked my questions more eloquently," Burchard said. "Would they have had authority to arrest either Mr. McGinnis or Mr. Hoffman for assault on a police officer or for resisting arrest?"

Price was hardly satisfied. He pressed his argument. "The Ferry County arrest warrant has so prejudiced the jury that such a taint cannot be remedied short of declaring a mistrial."

Gardner interjected, "This is the consequence of trying the two defendants together in the first place."

The jury reconvened after attorneys debated the matter for most of an afternoon. The judge instructed the panel to disregard the prosecutor's reference to an arrest warrant for Mr. Hoffman from the Ferry County District Court.

The flare-up over the arrest warrant produced a headline story in the *Wenatchee World* on what was termed "prosecutorial misconduct." Exchanges between Burchard and Price over the Ferry County warrant made provocative news copy.

Attorneys on both sides clearly understood what was at stake. Identifying Patrick as a fugitive could establish his motive for hauling the weapons over rugged terrain. From the state's perspective, both defendants were avoiding arrest. Patrick's exodus from the Impala at Armstrong Meadows and his backcountry route to reach home during early morning hours were evidence that he anticipated police were also looking for him. Both defendants were determined to shoot it out if necessary to avoid arrest. The defense argued that Patrick's arrest warrant was never in play during the shooting incident.

Chapter 18

Police Conduct

The bad press over charges of prosecutorial misconduct did not seem to faze the prosecutor going forward. Burchard's advocacy ratcheted up a notch, or so it seemed to defense attorneys, for the remainder of the trial.

The state wanted to establish that Elmer was primed to do battle with tribal police. To that end, Burchard called Councilman Kohler and Chief Smiskin as witnesses.

Dale Kohler was asked to take the stand. "Describe your position on the Tribal Business Council and your background," Burchard began.

"I'm an elected representative to the council from the Omak district. I have a degree in economics and received a law degree from Gonzaga University," Kohler said.

"What is the role of the council?"

"Basically, we govern the Colville Reservation of Confederated Tribes. We oversee external agencies involved in mining and timber, oversee public services of safety and law enforcement, and resolve enrollment issues," Kohler replied.

"How did you come to know Elmer McGinnis?"

"I've known Elmer for at least twelve years. Over the years, he's visited me regularly to talk about his concerns on the reservation."

"Let's turn to events on the afternoon of August 25 when Elmer contacted you at your office. When did you first see the defendant enter your office on that day?" Burchard asked.

"While speaking on the telephone to a fellow councilman, Mr. George, I happened to see McGinnis out my window, driving into the parking lot. It was around 3:00 p.m. I wasted no time in calling Chief Smiskin to tell him that Elmer McGinnis had just showed up," Kohler explained.

"Why did you call the police chief?"

"I made the call because there was a tribal court warrant of criminal trespass in the Keller district. Shortly after the phone call, two tribal police showed up, Officers Marconi and Whitney."

"What happened next?"

"The officers approached Elmer and told him they had an arrest warrant and he needed to come along with them. Elmer told them bluntly that they had no authority for the arrest. Elmer said he wanted to talk with me. I could sense from his hostile tone that Elmer was not going anywhere until he talked with me. I agreed to talk with him. He told me he wanted to register a complaint over how tribal police handled a car accident earlier in the day."

"What did he complain about?"

"A fifteen- to sixteen-year-old girl had been involved in an accident, and the tribal police had not acted quickly enough. I was aware of the incident, but told Elmer I felt the response time was very adequate," Kohler said. "About that time, Chief Smiskin arrived with a copy of the warrant and presented it to McGinnis. Elmer briefly glanced at the document, then wadded it up and threw it on the floor."

"What did Mr. McGinnis do next?"

"It was obvious that Elmer was not going to go willingly, so the officers took hold of him and tried to move him toward the door of my office. At that point, all hell broke out. Elmer fought against the officers, throwing his arms," Kohler answered.

"Did the officers strike or kick Elmer McGinnis?" asked Burchard.

"The officers did not hit or kick Elmer, but they did force him to the floor. Elmer threw himself forward, and the two officers fell on top of him, each officer holding one arm. As the officers attempted to put the cuffs on, Elmer yelled, 'Get your hands off me, you sons of bitches!'" Kohler responded.

"At that point, what did the officers do?"

"Then Elmer yelled about chest pains. He said he was having a heart attack. Chief Smiskin shouted at me to get an ambulance. I made contact with EMS. The officers and McGinnis struggled on the floor until the ambulance crew of Kelly Manley and Bill Joseph arrived. The crew tried to get Elmer on a stretcher, but he continued to throw his arms and kick with his legs, resisting efforts to subdue him. After several futile attempts to get him on the stretcher, police just picked him up and carried him bodily down the hallway. One officer had hold of his chest, and the other officer had him by the legs," Kohler said. "Wendell George, a fellow business council member, and John Smith with the Fish and Wildlife Department ran out to Elmer's pickup to get his medication. Wendell found two bottles in his truck and showed them to Elmer."

"How did the defendant respond when offered the medication?" asked the prosecutor.

"Seeing the pill bottles, Elmer became angrier and yelled, 'Get that goddamn thing out of here. Who got into my pickup? You had no authority to get into my pickup,'" Kohler said.

"That's all I have for the witness now," Burchard said.

The defense thoroughly vetted Dale Kohler over the police tactics used to subdue McGinnis. Richard Price repeatedly pressed Kohler over whether police had used abusive tactics, but Kohler did not waver in his testimony. No officer or first responder kicked or punched him.

Burchard called Chief Smiskin to the stand. Much of his testimony corroborated Kohler's version of events. He testified that Elmer was very combative, and police had used proper procedures when the defendant violently resisted arrest. Burchard skillfully directed the witness to affirm that no officer struck McGinnis or used abusive force when subduing the defendant.

In cross-examination, Bud Gardner asked Chief Smiskin, "What precipitated the use of physical constraints when exposing the arrest warrant?"

"After conducting business with Dale Kohler, Elmer was very agitated. His eyes twitched, and he showed other nervous mannerisms," replied Smiskin.

"Is it not true that you shoved Mr. McGinnis into file cabinets in the office?" asked Gardner. "To quote from an FBI report, 'I then shoved McGinnis into the black file cabinets, which he struck quite hard.'"

"No…I may have misspoken. Elmer fell to the floor on his left side. I asked Elmer to cooperate, that he should not resist while on the floor, but the resistance continued."

"Why did you transfer Elmer McGinnis to the Okanogan County Jail rather than the tribal jail?" Gardner continued.

"That was not an unusual procedure. Anyone who wanted to escape from the tribal jail could get out easily. I was also concerned about his heart condition. They had medical backup available at the Okanogan County Jail."

"I don't think I understand, Chief Smiskin. If you had concerns about the tribal jail, how you could conclude that McGinnis should be left without a guard at a nonsecure facility like a hospital?"

"Since a nurse was on duty and Elmer was connected to a heart monitor, we felt confident that he was secure. An alarm would sound if the machine was disconnected, alerting the nurse's station," Smiskin replied.

"I'm still confused," Gardner said. "If you were concerned about housing him in the tribal jail, what was it about the hospital that made you feel otherwise?"

"I felt that Elmer must have had a medical problem and was not going anywhere," Chief Smiskin replied.

Given the lateness of the Friday afternoon, the judge adjourned the trial.

≑ ≑ ≑

The following Monday, March 2, Richard Price opened his cross-examination of the police chief by questioning how the arrest warrant was served to Elmer McGinnis. "Why had you, as the chief tribal officer, not served the bench warrant prior to the encounter in Dale Kohler's office?" he asked.

Mr. Hicks objected. "There is no foundation for the question, and counsel is asking a leading question."

"Mr. Price, please refrain from the use of leading questions," admonished the judge.

Price rephrased his question. "McGinnis had lodged complaints to the witness from time to time about shootings at his premises, presumably without permission, but no action was taken. Is this not correct?"

"Your honor, I strongly object. May we have a sidebar?" asked Hicks.

"Come forward," replied the judge. Attorneys debated the question of whether such evidence on the defendant had been properly introduced.

"I am going to sustain the objection. Mr. Price, you're putting matters before the jury that this witness hasn't testified to and may or may not have knowledge of…it just doesn't seem that it's proper cross-examination."

"If Elmer McGinnis was such a dangerous individual, why did police not make an arrest when the warrant was issued? The tribal police—they were very, very on the edge about something. Why were police taking actions like raiding the McGinnis residence and not others like making a simple arrest earlier?" Price asked.

For Richard Price, Chief Smiskin was avoiding the obvious answer. The chief law enforcement officer, councilmen, and mental health professionals wanted no part of dealing with Elmer McGinnis. His threats and arsenal of weapons were well known.

"You need to establish a foundation before going forward with this line of questioning. Objection is affirmed," the judge repeated.

Price rephrased his question. "Why did you and Kohler repeatedly focus on the dangerousness of Elmer McGinnis?"

Burchard objected. "Counsel's questions are outside the scope, subject to speculation, and leading."

"Objection sustained," said the judge.

"Turning to events on the morning of August twenty-seventh after one o'clock a.m., what aims did police hope to accomplish, if anything, after the search had been called off?" asked Price.

Both Hicks and Burchard objected.

Price called for a sidebar. "It is very difficult to track my thoughts with two prosecutors continually objecting. As a courtesy, could objections be limited to the attorney conducting direct examination of the witness?"

"That's reasonable," Hicks answered. "We will abide by your restriction."

On another matter, Price complained, "I have seen Chief Smiskin and FBI Agent Jim Davis talking together with Mr. Burchard. Witnesses are not to discuss their testimony with other witnesses."

"Special Agent Davis is what we call the case agent for the state. He did not have a conversation about his testimony with the prosecutor, nor did Chief Smiskin," claimed Hicks.

The judge cut off arguments. "Let me be clear—to both parties. Witnesses are not to discuss their in-court testimony with any other potential witnesses."

Price concluded his cross-examination with questions about the witness's knowledge of a call made to Officer Millard on the early morning of the twenty-seventh, and the amount of time required to return from Keller back to the McGinnis residence. Chief Smiskin estimated that approximately a half hour to forty-five minutes was needed to make the return trip to Nespelem.

Mr. Hicks, on redirect, asked, "When had police noticed shadows near the house?"

"It was around two a.m. Phillips made a call," Smiskin replied.

"Who was in charge on the evening of the twenty-sixth?" Hicks asked.

"Sergeant Millard was in charge that evening with Assistant Chief John Dick second in command," Smiskin said.

"What did you instruct Officer Phillips to do if he saw anyone in the area?" asked Hicks.

"If Officer Phillips observed anything, he was to notify dispatch, and dispatch would notify officers that had been sent home," explained Smiskin.

"That's all I have," Hicks announced.

At the end of nearly two days of testimony, the police chief welcomed the judge's announcement that he could step down.

Chapter 19

Family Loyalty

Prosecutors counted on Elmer's eldest daughter, Francis Peoples, to provide key testimony as to Elmer's remarks while leaving the Impala at Armstrong Meadows and identify the gym bag and weapons removed from the car. Under the terms of a plea agreement, Francis had agreed to offer her testimony as a witness for the state. FBI Agent Edmund Burke had interviewed her in the tribal jail on the morning after the shoot-out, August 27.

After her arrest, Francis got little sleep on the hard bunk of the tribal jail. She remained very worried about her father and brother. In mid-morning a well-dressed stranger appeared.

"Hi. I am Edmund Burke, an FBI agent. Here are my credentials."

"Do you have any word about my dad and my brother?" Francis asked.

Burke summarized what he knew at the time. "Your dad and brother were involved in a shoot-out with tribal police at your dad's place. Your dad was hit and is in critical condition at Grand Coulee Hospital. Two tribal officers were also victims; one was killed and the other is hospitalized. Your brother is still at large."

"That's awful," Francis said as her eyes swelled with tears.

"Yes, it is tragic. I am here this morning to ask questions about what you observed the last couple of days. Is that okay?" Burke asked.

"I have nothing to offer. I wasn't there… Is Dad gonna make it?"

"I do not know at this point. All we know is that he survived. For now, you can help by giving us details of what happened before the shootout erupted."

"I'd rather not."

"Here's the deal. You will likely face charges of aiding and abetting the escape of your father. If you cooperate, there is the possibility that these charges could be reduced or eliminated if you were to offer truthful testimony," Burke said.

Without the benefit of an attorney, Francis thought it over and reluctantly agreed to the interview. Her first priority was to be released from jail and make contacts with her children and sisters.

Hesitantly, Francis came forward and took a seat in the witness chair. Hicks approached the witness stand. "Will the witness please give her name?"

"My name is Francis Peoples."

"Where do you live?"

"I live in Keller, Washington. I am a single woman, and I have four children."

"Are you currently employed?"

"No."

"What is your relationship to Patrick Hoffman?"

"He's my brother. He's the young man seated at the table with an off-white jacket," Francis said. His handsome image was hard to ignore; it stood in stark contrast to the mug shots—with long hair, a beard, and a scowl—offered in news accounts.

"What living arrangements do you have with your brother Patrick Hoffman?"

"He has lived with me for about three years," Peoples replied.

"When you and the McGinnis family visited Mid-Valley Hospital, were you not aware that your father, Elmer McGinnis, was under arrest?" asked Hicks.

"I was not sure what his status was."

"Did you and your family visit Prosecutor Bob Widdifield?"

"Yes. He told us Dad was in the hospital."

"Is that all he told you? Isn't it true that he told you what happened at the council office—that your father resisted arrest?" Hicks asked.

"Yes…that police got in a fight with Dad when they tried to arrest him," Peoples said.

"Why did you visit the tribal prosecutor?"

"We wanted to find out why Dad was arrested and whether we could visit him at the hospital," Peoples responded.

"Did Patrick Hoffman have a gym bag with him on the morning of the twenty-sixth?"

"I don't know."

"Did you ever see Patrick Hoffman carrying a black gym bag?"

"When we went on Pat's motorcycle, he usually carried the gym bag."

"Did he ever carry weapons in the gym bag?"

"He carried a forty-five," said Peoples.

"Were there other weapons in the gym bag?"

"He had a twenty-two pistol Dad gave to Pat and me, but I don't know if it was in the bag. Usually he leaves it at home because it's an antique."

The judge requested a fifteen-minute break to allow the court reporter to put in another tape. Near the end of the break, Bud Gardner approached the bench and requested a sidebar. "Your Honor, Vicki Ross, who is a witness for the state, was observed discussing matters with state witnesses in the hallway during recesses." Vicki Ross, Sergeant Millard's life partner, had been asked to testify as to her contact with him prior to his tragic death. Of interest to the defense, the 9-millimeter semiautomatic found in Sergeant Millard's police car allegedly belonged to Vicki Ross. "Since Miss Ross is still under subpoena for the defense, my client sees this as a violation of his rights under the Indian Civil Rights Act," Gardner said.

Hicks quickly interjected, "Whether he feels it's a violation has no bearing upon the court's orders, unless the defense makes some showing of inappropriate comments by this witness. It's up to Bud Gardner to put it on the record. Let's not make these blind statements. That's part of Mr. McGinnis's problems for a number of years—he thinks he can just say things, and the court will take them at face value." Hicks raised his voice. "Why would counsel introduce such an objection when he knew it was baseless and unfounded? We object to this continued harangue at our witnesses merely because the defense is keeping them under subpoena, too, for whatever purposes."

Gardner replied, "There was no intention to intimidate or harass state witnesses. It's a question of appearance of fairness."

Hicks countered, "While I do not wish to incite counsel, why has the defense subpoenaed so many witnesses without updating them as to their status? We're seeing witnesses calling Mr. Price's office, asking, 'When am I going to testify?' and things like that, and getting no response."

Price responded angrily, "There's no proof of that, and I'm damn mad about the state suggesting that we're harassing people by subpoenaing them. That's our right to subpoena witnesses," he said. "These people are on trial as defendants for murder, and by God we're going to subpoena everybody we want to."

Judge Alumbaugh calmly interrupted, "The court has not responded to such allegations, Mr. Price, nor will I do so in the future. I will restrict my ruling to Miss Ross and other witnesses. All witnesses need to clear the hallways during recess and any kind of break, at the end of the day or at the noon hour. There's only one door to the courtroom, making the hallway a place to visit. I'm asking attorneys to advise all witnesses to not congregate and discuss testimony in the area. It is also a security concern," the judge said. Attorneys said they would comply, and the trial resumed.

Hicks picked up the gym bag and showed it to Francis Peoples. "Does this bag belong to Patrick Hoffman?"

"Yes," Francis said.

"Did Patrick Hoffman have ownership of this bag on August twenty-sixth, 1986?"

"Yes, this is the same bag he owned then, but I'm not sure this bag was with him on the day we visited the hospital," Francis said.

"Were you arrested on the night of August twenty-sixth?" Hicks asked.

"Yes, I was. But they never told us why we were stopped and arrested."

"When did you meet FBI Agent Ed Burke?"

"Police put me in the tribal jail, and this FBI guy met me that morning," Francis replied.

"Did Agent Burke bring this bag with him, and did he ask you to identify it?" Hicks asked.

"Yeah. It is Pat's. The guy showed it to me and pulled some articles of clothing out of it."

"Did you make a statement to Agent Burke that Patrick Hoffman had that bag with him while at the hospital?"

"I cannot recall his question or my answer."

Hicks then exposed a handgun to the witness. After marking it as an exhibit, Hicks asked Francis if she had seen the weapon before.

"It looks like the one that my father gave Pat and me," she said. Upon further inquiry, she identified the gun as a .22 pistol and stated that she had not fired the weapon or purchased ammunition for it. Hicks introduced a second weapon for identification. "It's a forty-five, the type that is loaded with a clip," Francis said. She also acknowledged that she had previously shot the gun.

"Did Patrick Hoffman own this gun?" asked Hicks.

"Yes. Pat has owned the gun ever since he has lived with me."

"Did he regularly carry the forty-five semiautomatic in the gym bag?"

"He regularly carried it in his gym bag," Francis said.

Hicks opened the bag. "Can you identify the gloves in the bag?"

Price strongly objected and called for a sidebar. "There is no way to verify where items came from, or even whether the items were in the bag when it was recovered," he protested.

Hicks answered, "I have only exposed the items to help the witness identify the bag. Foundations for the objects in the bag will be established later."

Burchard complained, "The witness has been granted immunity. Earlier she admitted to Agent Burke that Hoffman had this bag at the hospital. She's obviously hostile…she refused to talk with me earlier, on December first. Now she's wavering on her testimony."

Inconsistencies in Peoples's testimony were overlooked momentarily. The judge ruled that items could not be removed from the bag. "Counsel may expose the inside of the bag to determine if the belongings and bag are defendant Hoffman's."

Hicks continued with the bag in hand. "Are any of the contents familiar?"

Francis quietly answered, "Some of the items in the bag are mine, and the other items belong to Pat."

Hicks held up a gun belt. "Are you familiar with this belt?"

"That's Pat's belt. He packed his forty-five in it."

"Did you see Patrick with the same gym bag on August twenty-sixth?"

"No, I do not recall seeing him with the bag."

In pretrial, Francis had acknowledged that the bag was in the car and that Patrick removed the bag before trekking down the valley toward the McGinnis residence. She also told FBI Agent Burke what was in the bag. In the agent's final report, Francis said Patrick had, among other items, three guns in the gym bag. In addition to the .22 pistol and .45 semiautomatic, Hoffman carried a 9-millimeter assault pistol.

The prosecutor shifted to her account of leaving the hospital and separating from her dad and brother. "When Patrick took the side road to Armstrong Meadows, why did he stop the car?" Hicks asked.

"Dad said he wanted to get out of the car," Francis said.

"What did your dad say before exiting the car?"

"I don't remember exactly what he said, only that he was afraid that us kids would get hurt with him being in the car."

"Are you sure you can't remember what he said?" Hicks pressed.

"Yes…I don't recall anything else."

"Didn't you tell FBI Agent Burke that your dad warned you and your sisters about staying out of the line of fire?"

"I don't remember saying that to the FBI guy. I said something about Dad being concerned that us girls would get hit if we all stayed in the car with Dad," Francis replied quietly.

"When Patrick left the car and joined your dad, did he have his gym bag at that time?"

"I don't recall seeing Pat with the gym bag at that time."

"You don't recall making such a remark to FBI Agent Ed Burke?"

"That's right."

"You don't recall saying that your dad told your family that he would rather die than go back to jail?"

"I don't know exactly how it was said. And I don't remember Dad saying he would rather die than go back to jail. It's been so long since I talked with this FBI guy, I don't remember what all was asked or what all was said."

Judge Alumbaugh announced a recess for lunch. She requested that the attorneys come forward to address her concerns. "I have no idea what this witness has told an FBI agent, but she clearly said something different when she was on the stand during the 3.5, 3.6 hearings.[1] I am uncomfortable with the implications of hearing the witness now state under oath that she has no recollection of such a statement. I don't want her to get into a perjury problem."

"Francis Peoples is not our witness. It's not our problem. The defense has no control over her testimony," Price responded.

"Well, the witness needs a counsel regarding her testimony," the judge said.

Hicks after returning from lunch resumed his examination, opening the bag. "Do you recognize any of these items?"

"I recognize this as Pat's back brace and a hair brush...the swimsuit belongs to me and the bandanna belongs to Pat. The flashlight, the one from fire control, also belongs to Pat," Francis said.

"What else do you recognize?" Hicks asked.

---

1   Pretrial hearings where the court examines the state's evidence of confessions (3.5) and reviews for possible suppression (3.6).

"I recognize the holster Pat made for the twenty-two. The black scarf and those things—maybe called sticks. They were Pat's. I don't know what the orange boxes are."

"What other weapons other than the twenty-two revolver and forty-five semiautomatic were in the bag when Patrick left the car?"

"I don't recall. I didn't look in his bag."

"I want to remind you, you were granted immunity based on you giving honest and truthful testimony. Are you sure you don't recall what you told Agent Burke?" Hicks asked.

"I object in the strongest terms. We need to have a sidebar," Price said. At the bench he continued, "The prosecutor only voiced the conditions for Francis Peoples's testimony to impeach the witness. A statement of immunity for the witness is highly prejudicial. It implied that the witness had committed a criminal act connected to his client. The primary reason the state granted her immunity was to get her to testify against one of the participants in this act."

The judge briefly listened to the subsequent colloquy over the propriety of introducing the terms of a plea agreement to a jury, then cut off the debate. "Prosecutors are not to say any more about immunity or truthfulness in your examination of the witness."

Hicks then directed his questioning to types and colors of jackets given to Patrick and Elmer. Francis confirmed their identity. Hicks said he had no further questions.

Gardner's cross-examination established that Francis and her sisters were not involved in any escape attempt from the hospital. Their aim was to help Elmer McGinnis reach home safely.

Francis was excused. An attorney was appointed to represent her for the remainder of the trial. The state had failed to shake their key witness's testimony—that she had in fact heard her father tell his daughters to stay out of the line of fire before exiting the Impala at Armstrong Meadows. Francis also failed to corroborate the presence of the 9-millimeter alleged murder weapon in Hoffman's gym bag. Such testimony was needed to confirm Burke's FBI report that McGinnis and Hoffman had anticipated a gun battle with police. It would also be a major element in the first-degree murder charge, showing that the defendants had formed intent to use deadly force when and if encountering tribal police.

Chapter 20

Gun Battle

The next morning, prosecutors called John Dick to the stand. The courtroom was crowded and boisterous; his testimony was long awaited. The defense team had a number of questions for the witness. After the loss of his friend and partner Sergeant Millard, Dick was treated for PTSD at Fairfax Hospital in Seattle, then convalesced at a Catholic retreat in Montana. Defense attorneys' efforts to serve him a subpoena during this time had proved futile.

Before Dick stepped up to the witness stand, Price asked for a sidebar. "I am disturbed by what could have been jury contamination. While eating lunch at the Cariboo Restaurant, local attorneys were talking about the trial in the presence of jurors taking their lunch break. I fear jurors may have overheard their take on the trial."

Bud Gardner seconded Price's concern. "I have also witnessed the same potential contamination. Attorneys asked me questions about the trial in the presence of three or four jurors sitting about ten feet away." Jurors had dispersed to at least three restaurants: the Cariboo, the Sawtooth, and the Cedars.

"I am also alarmed at jury lunch arrangements," Judge Alumbaugh replied. "I worry that other patrons may interact with jurors, offering their own views of the proceedings. This is a worrisome arrangement that needs to be corrected. Henceforth, jurors will eat together in one area and be isolated from other patrons if feasible." The next day, jurors agreed on one restaurant and had their lunch in a conference room for the remainder of the trial.

Burchard asked Dick to step forward as a witness. Dick's steps were measured. He adjusted his position in the witness chair and wiped slight perspiration off his brow.

"Good Morning," Burchard said. "Could you provide the jury your name for the record?"

He replied quietly, "My name is John Dick."

"What was your employment history with the tribal force?" asked Burchard.

"My last full-time employment was as Assistant Chief of Police at the Colville Confederated Tribes. I think I started in 1979, and ended my duties January of 1987. I was commissioned as Okanogan Deputy Sheriff, and also held a commission with the Bureau of Indian Affairs."

"What position did you hold at the time of the shooting incident?"

"I was second in the chain of command, having administrative and supervisory duties."

"Where are you presently employed?"

"Right now I'm a student and live in St. Ignatius, Montana. I took a leave right after the shooting and resigned in January."

"Do you have a family?"

"Yes. I'm married and the father of two children."

Sensitive to the difficulty of recalling the tragic moments during the shoot-out, Burchard asked, "How would you describe your relationship with Sergeant Lou Millard?"

"He was my closest friend and my ride-along companion. We made a lot of calls together…we trusted each other." Dick took a deep breath. "Our lives depended on it. Lou was the kind of officer you wanted to have your back. We made dangerous calls sometimes." Dick's eyes moistened. "I trusted Lou. We worked well as a team."

"Can we talk about what happened?" asked Burchard.

"Sure," Dick said, raising his head slightly.

"What plans did you make around midnight in your search for the de-fendants?"

"It was getting late. The chief had asked Lou and me, along with Ser-geant Carden, Deputy Sheriff Tom McCone, and State Patrol Officer Greg Minzer, to gather at his office. We talked over whether we should stay in pursuit or call it off."

"What did you decide?"

"We all agreed with Chief Smiskin. We should call it a night for the coordinated manhunt. The chief said it was pretty dangerous doing a search at night in the mountains. Chief Smiskin reasoned it was best to do the search at daybreak, and try to get a helicopter up."

"Then what happened?"

"All of us were sent home except Officers Brian Phillips and Chester Clark. They were assigned to watch the McGinnis property to see if Elmer and Pat might show up. I headed back home to Elmer City, about ten to twelve miles south of Nespelem. About 1:45 a.m., the phone rang and woke me. The dispatcher informed me that Officer Phillips had spotted two individuals walking under a street lamp toward the McGinnis property."

"How long did it take you to reach the scene?"

"I got there fairly quickly. It didn't take long to get my gear on, my Sec-ond Chance vest and my uniform. I headed north toward Cache Creek Road and turned toward the McGinnis place. I drove to the corrals on the west side of the McGinnis house. Other patrol cars were parked near a pole fence," Dick said.

"Would you please point out on this diagram where you parked your car?"

Price objected. "This is not an accurate representation of the area in question, and therefore I challenge the question of Officer Dick's car in his testimony."

"I request a sidebar on this and another matter," Burchard said.

The judge was impatient over defense objections to the chart. "The court isn't going to rule any further on counsel's objection to the demonstrative evidence. A record has been made on that." The judge had ruled the diagram could be used for illustration purposes only.

On the other matter, Burchard asked the judge, "Would you rule on our motion that John Dick's subsequent psychiatric treatment after the shootings be considered privileged information? The Washington State Patrol conducts a program to treat officers for possible PTSD from traumatic encounters in the line of duty. Accordingly, Chief Smiskin recommended that Officer Dick seek this treatment. If the court rules that such treatment is open to inquiry, the ruling may discourage future officers from participating in this program."

"Mr. Dick's state of mind that evening and morning is at the core of what really happened. What was his attitude when arriving at the scene?" Price said. "The question of specific inquiries into psychiatric areas is dependent upon the testimony Dick provides."

Judge Alumbaugh interjected, "No one has challenged Mr. Dick's competency to testify. Thus, Mr. Dick's treatment or counseling for post-traumatic effects is collateral and really not relevant." The judge directed her remarks to Mr. Burchard: "And that is as some direction to the prosecutor."

Burchard resumed questioning the witness. "What did tribal officers find, if anything, when surveilling the two abandoned houses?"

"I and Officers Millard, Phillips, and Carden checked out the houses and found nothing."

"Did any officer draw his weapon during the search?"

"Each of us drew his gun before entering each house."

"What actions did you take after securing the two abandoned houses?"

"We then decided to check out an abandoned pickup east of the house. Three of us split off; Lou Millard, Brian Phillips and me made our way to the pickup. Along the way, I grew very concerned about the floodlights from the emergency vehicle parked on Cache Creek Road, which lit up most of the McGinnis property. The backlighting made us easy targets. I told the EMT, Bill Joseph, to turn the lights off."

"What did you find near the pickup?"

"We looked around the pickup and inside the cab and along the north fence line. We didn't come up with anything. I could see a little trail south of the pickup. Lou and I followed the path toward a fence, which was just outside the backyard. I led the way with Lou behind. I crawled over the fence while Lou held it down. We joked about having to lose a little weight if we were going to make a habit of going over barbed-wire fences," Dick said.

"Why did you and Officer Millard decide to cross the fence?"

"I wanted to secure the area."

"What were your thoughts at the time?"

"My first thought was that the two individuals seen under the street light were a couple of drunks. I had passed by the War Bonnet on the way to the McGinnis house, and it was not unusual to see people walking home at that late hour. But I also thought it could be Elmer and Patrick," Dick said.

"I object. His thoughts are not appropriate evidence," Price said.

"Objection sustained. Move on to another area," the judge ruled.

Burchard was not to be deterred from his line of questioning. "I insist the jury be removed to challenge this objection," he said, and the judge so ordered. Looking directly at Price, Burchard argued, "His thoughts are relevant as to his intent." Turning his attention to the judge, he said, "The defense has made a claim that Officer Dick went to the house to pick up a couple of drunks because he thought the defendants had not had enough time to get to the house. All of this has to do with police intention. While he may have thought it could be a couple of drunks, he still thought it should be checked out."

"Isn't that what he was responding to?" the judge asked.

"He was not allowed to," Burchard complained. "My next question was, 'How did you arrive at that conclusion?'"

The judge ruled that if Burchard rephrased the question to ask what Dick was thinking earlier in the evening or at another time, that would be allowed. The defense was not pleased. Their objection was clear, given the self-defense argument. The police had no clear plan of action when entering the McGinnis property. Police had first thought the two who crossed Cache Creek Road were drunks. Price asked later, did police narrative change after the fact?

Continuing his examination, the prosecutor asked, "Once you arrived at the scene, what were your thoughts about the dispatch report of seeing two men cross Cache Creek Road?"

"I was thinking at the time that they didn't have enough time to hike seven or eight miles from Great Western Lake to Nespelem. That's why I thought it might be a couple of drunks, but I made sure and checked it out," Dick replied.

"What did you and Officer Millard do after crossing into the McGinnis backyard?"

"Before going over the fence, we flashed our flashlights on the east side of the McGinnis house. We saw nothing moving, so I told Sergeant Millard, 'Let's go check out that area—the chicken coop and behind it.'"

"Did you draw your weapons during the search?"

"Both of us had our revolvers holstered when going into the yard," Dick said.

"Did you know the location of Officers Carden and Phillips at that time?"

"Yes. Looking behind me, I could see Officers Carden and Phillips. They were walking in front of their patrol car lights."

"Describe your actions once you were in the McGinnis backyard."

"As I said before, we joked over losing some pounds if we had to cross any more fences. We laughed and made our way toward the southwest area of the yard. We heard a noise while walking toward the south fence, and we flashed our lights in the direction of the commotion. Both of us were relieved to spot a black or dark-colored horse looking at us."

"What happened next?"

"After seeing it was a horse, we moved up the incline of the yard toward the chicken coop on the southwestern corner of the property. My intention was to check it out. I walked up to the end of the chicken coop on the east side, and I leaned over to look on the north side. I directed my flashlight toward the upper half of the building. I was looking for any opened doors."

"Had you drawn your revolver?"

"I still had my service revolver holstered at that time." Dick paused and then added, "I observed nothing. I flashed my light to the other side, the back of the building. I started to turn. I don't know if I took one or two steps. Nothing was there, so I turned to walk back down the hill. As I turned my upper body, I noticed an orange flash over my left shoulder and a pop. It was like a firecracker, like a rifle, like a weapon report." Dick hesitated, recalling the moment. "I felt a stinging in my back, like a big bee sting. When I got hit, I started to fall. I yelled at Lou that I was hit. Lou yelled back, 'John, if you're hit, get down.'"

"Where was Lou Millard?"

"Lou was opposite the flash I saw, north of the chicken coop."

"What happened next?"

"I went down, I guess, due to being hit. I dropped my light and grabbed my right arm. The light was still on. I fell on my stomach with my head facing north. The next thing I observed was more gunfire over me. I don't know from what direction. I had my head covered." Dick paused again to regain his thoughts. "Then it got quiet—real quiet. The next thing I noticed was a flare going up, a popping-type flare that illuminated the area. I did not look up. Next, I heard more gunfire. I heard bullets hitting the ground, but I didn't know where they were coming from."

"Did you know where Lou Millard was at that moment?" asked Burchard.

"Not really. I did hear Lou moaning. He was down the hill toward the northeast. I started crawling toward him on the ground. While I crawled, another flare went up. I drew my gun. I heard more firing coming from behind me. I could hear the bullets thunking, but I didn't know where they were hitting. I still couldn't see Lou. Finally, the shooting started to die down, and I crawled further down the sloped yard and found Lou. I could hear him moaning. I crawled from where I first saw his feet to the left-hand side of him."

"What did you do next?"

"Lou was lying on his face with his stomach facing south. I tried to talk with him, asking, 'How bad are you hit?' He didn't answer. He just made a gurgling sound." Dick struggled to continue. He took another deep breath. "I looked for some cover for us. I noticed a concrete piling to the east. I could see it because of a fire burning over there. The fire was headed our way. I was trying to drag Lou toward the foundation with my right arm by his belt, but he was pretty heavy. I don't know if I moved him at all. All I know is I didn't get us to cover behind the cement foundation."

Burchard waited as Dick wiped his tears. "Can you tell us what happened next?"

"One more flare was shot. It went up and came down. It lit up the area where Lou and I were and then slowly came down, lighting up the whole yard. As the flare hit the ground, more gunfire came from the east side of the chicken coop. I could see orange flashes in that direction."

"How did you respond?"

"It was then that I pulled my revolver and started firing where I saw the flashes. I emptied my gun at them just to make them stop shooting at us."

"Could you tell who was shooting at you?"

"I had the impression that one person was shooting the flares and another was firing guns. At that point I holstered my gun. I tried again to get Lou to the cement foundation but could not budge him with my good arm. Another flare was shot, and more gunfire was directed at us."

"Did you fire your weapon in response?"

"I grabbed the speed loader for my revolver. I was prepared to go down fighting if they came out from behind the coop to finish us off," Dick said. "I crawled next to Lou and told him I was going for help. I yelled a number of times, 'Somebody help us,' and no one answered. I yelled as loud as I could. I didn't know where any of the other officers were at that time. When I left Lou, he had been hit, but he appeared to be alive. I thought he was trying to talk to me when I asked him how bad he had been hit; he just couldn't talk.

"I stumbled down the hill for help. I saw another flare go up and heard more shooting. I held my head down. I was facing downhill. The shooting was coming behind me toward the south. I crawled to the fence where we went over into the yard. I looked back up on the hill. I thought I saw someone jump in the bushes from behind the chicken coop. I couldn't identify who it was."

"Describe where you headed next," said Burchard.

"I crawled over the fence north of the old pickup. I called for help and fell down. Nobody came down to where I was. I called for help again, and again nobody came. I got up, walked a ways, and fell down again. I called for help again, and that's when Sergeant Carden came out from a car and grabbed me. It was Lou Millard's squad car."

"What did you say to Sergeant Carden?"

"I told him to get back up the hill and help Lou, that Lou was hit badly. He ignored my order and continued to pull me to a nearby police car. He then helped me lie down on the pavement. Sergeant Carden got in the car and tried to contact the dispatcher for help, but the radio was not working."

"Did Officer Carden make radio contact?"

"Yes, he finally got through. My pain was pretty bad, but most of all I was upset that Officer Carden and others failed to provide backup and rescue Lou. After updating the office, Carden got out of his car, helped me to my feet, and placed me in the back seat."

"And where did Sergeant Carden take you?"

"He drove toward an ambulance parked on Cache Creek Road. I yelled at him to turn around and get back up the hill to provide cover for Lou."

"Did he stop the car?"

"No. He continued to drive Sergeant Millard's police car to the ambulance."

"Where were you sent?"

"I was transferred to Grand Coulee Hospital."

"What treatment did you receive?"

"They stitched me up, and I was hospitalized until Friday, about three days. I went back three times to have everything checked out. The wound healed fairly well. My arm feels good and I can move it around pretty good."

The prosecutor said that was all he had for this round.

Price had waited months for this opportunity. John Dick had not responded to defense subpoenas. Was this a cover-up? Price wanted answers as to what actually happened when Dick was hit by a bullet and who may have fired the initial volley.

Price began his cross-examination by asking about Elmer's arrest warrant. "Did you have any contact with individual complainants in the lands trespass charge prior to the shooting incident on the twenty-seventh?"

"Donnie Ferguson contacted me earlier that morning...the twenty-sixth as I recall, telling me to call him if Elmer was ever released from jail. He wanted to know so he could move his family out of the area because he was afraid for his family. I was fearful for his family if Elmer got past us, and I knew we'd have trouble. He had kicked one of the officers when we tried to arrest him, and he had a gun when he went to Indian Health Services," Dick replied.

Counsel shifted to the night of August 26. "Why were so many officers called into duty to seek out Elmer McGinnis?"

"It was a dangerous situation. That's why I called in officers to try to locate him," Dick said with urgency.

"Why was Officer Phillips assigned to do surveillance on the McGinnis property after the search had been called off by Chief Smiskin?" asked Price.

"Chief Smiskin made the call. It was after he had consulted with officers gathered in his office about 11:30 p.m. The chief ordered Clark and Phillips to surveil the McGinnis house. The remaining officers were sent home to continue the search in the morning. We were all pretty tired. It was dangerous searching the mountainous area at night."

"So you really did not have a plan that night, correct?"

"We didn't have a plan that night. I agree."

"Is it not standard police procedure in dangerous situations to have a plan and know the location of all officers at the scene?"

"It's important to know where your fellow officers are and coordinate efforts when doing a dangerous search."

"Were you aware that Elmer McGinnis thought police were out to get him?" asked Price.

"I've known over the years. Elmer mistrusted the tribal police."

"Did you make any announcement while near or on the McGinnis property that you were law officers and you intended to make an arrest?" Price followed.

"We didn't announce our presence when arriving at the McGinnis place because we didn't believe there was anybody on the premises."

"So why were you on the McGinnis property?" Price testily asked.

"I was on the property to clear the area and search it, to see if Mr. McGinnis was there and to arrest him for escape from custody. I didn't know his doctor had discharged him."

Shifting his line of questioning, Price asked, "Where did the bullet that hit you enter your body? I remind you that you told the treating physician that you did not know what direction the bullet came from."

"I took a couple of steps, and I felt this large bee sting. I couldn't tell what direction the bullet was coming from."

Burchard loudly said, "I object to the line of questioning." He turned to the judge. "I request a sidebar." The request was granted. "A witness cannot be impeached with someone else's report. A witness cannot be expected to read someone else's report and interpret it."

Price countered, "I asked Mr. Dick to clarify what he meant by the direction of the bullet that hit him. Reports to the FBI agent and Dr. Sheldon, who treated his wound, were aids in refreshing the witness's memory. This tactic is no different than what was used on Francis Peoples!"

Judge Alumbaugh removed her glasses. "Enough already…if a report is read in front of the jury and that's not his statement, that would be improper," she said. "If counsel gives the witness a copy of a report to refresh his memory, that's one thing, but if you ask the witness in front of the jury something like, 'Didn't you tell somebody something else?' I don't think that's proper." The judge added, "Give the witness a copy of whatever, and let him look at it, and see if it refreshes his memory. That would be proper."

Price answered with some effrontery to the judge and Burchard. "If the state knows everything that happened and this witness knows everything, there is probably no reason for me to be up here taking the court's time and the jury's time cross-examining." Price paused for a moment, and continued with apparent exasperation. "My effort in this line of questioning is to get to the truth of what happened. The medical record will be introduced to show John Dick's remarks to the doctor who treated his wound. This isn't impeachment. This is trying to get at the truth of what happened."

Burchard said, "It's a question of the rules of evidence. What I'm objecting to is giving the witness somebody else's report and making him read it out loud to the jury."

The judge intervened and repeated her ruling. "Having the witness read another account aloud is improper if the purpose is to impeach the witness with another's report."

The disappointed defense counsel continued his cross-examination. "What did you tell Dr. Sheldon about the direction of the bullet that hit you?"

"I was in considerable pain at the time. I don't recall what I told Dr. Sheldon regarding whether I was shot from the front or back," Dick replied.

"When shot, what did you see? Could you give us more detail?" Price asked.

"When I got shot, I grabbed myself where the pain was, looking at my arm. That's when Lou yelled, 'John, if you're hit, get down.'"

"Could you actually see Lou Millard?"

"It's true I did not see Lou at that time. He wasn't standing next to me."

Price shifted to the type of ammunition he may have had loaded in his police-issued revolver. "Did you load your weapon with hollow-point bullets rather than fully jacketed bullets?"

"No. No, sir."

"As it turned out, there was another weapon belonging to Mr. Millard at the scene that evening, wasn't there?"

Burchard vehemently objected, "It's a complete misstatement. Counsel needs to be admonished in the absence of a jury." The judge asked attorneys to approach the bench. Mr. Burchard made his objection clearer. "Questions offered to mislead the jury, such as suggesting there was another weapon belonging to Lou Millard, are improper."

Judge Alumbaugh agreed. "While the defense needs latitude, this is not a proper line of inquiry. Basically, Mr. Price, you are asking this witness about his knowledge of what somebody else may have reported. Also, questioning the witness about using hollow-points as opposed to fully jacketed bullets is simply telling the jury counsel's point of view about such ammunition."

"We are defending against a charge of murder. There was another weapon on the scene, and it was a 9-millimeter," Price said with growing frustration. "I am entitled to ask about another weapon and how it got into a vehicle, because it is a key element to establish who was shooting what."

"So, you want to ask Mr. Dick if there were other weapons at the scene?" the judge asked.

"Yes, specifically whether or not he knew that Mr. Millard had a 9-millimeter," Price said.

Mr. Burchard challenged the premise. "Both the state and defense experts examined the gun in Mr. Millard's car and determined that it was not related to the bullets recovered from Mr. McGinnis and Sergeant Millard or the 9-millimeter bullet recovered in a field."

Price rebutted, "I did not read the reports that way."

The judge saw that this was not the time to arbitrate forensic evidence. It was up to the state to prove which weapon was fired at whom. Rather than further debate this point, the judge said, "Mr. Price, please continue your cross-examination."

With no explanation, Price declined and sat down. His frustration was apparent. The court had not offered more leeway to pursue his theory that one of the tribal officers had fired a 9-millimeter weapon during the shooting, killing Millard.

Mr. Gardner rose and pressed John Dick, "Were you aware of the 9-millimeter found in Lou Millard's police car?"

"I was unaware of the presence of the 9-millimeter," Dick answered.

"That's all for now," Gardner said.

"Court will be in recess and reconvene at one thirty," the judge announced.

After the lunch break, Burchard requested a sidebar. "Your Honor, a problem came up that I wanted to bring to your attention. Just after our recess, I was walking out with Mr. Dick and he was served with a subpoena by the defense. We walked down the hall a while, and I reacted inappropriately. I took the subpoena from him and brought it back, threw it on Mr. Price's table, and told Mr. Price to get fucked. I said that in a low voice. I don't know if Mr. Price heard it or not. It was not in the presence of the court or the jury. The court may determine that I should be disciplined for that, or counsel may wish, or the court may wish, to refer to the Bar Association, and I thought I should bring it to your attention."

"I did not intend to raise it," Price said.

"Mr. Dick acknowledged that he was served," Burchard said. "I became aware that that was the first opportunity the defense had to serve him. I was way out of line. I thought he had been served."

Judge Alumbaugh said, "Well, I appreciate you bringing it to the court's attention. You are absolutely right. It was totally inappropriate. And that's all I'm going to say about it. Now, Mr. Gardner, you have something to add?"

"I just want to say that it was over my shoulder. I had no idea what was going on, so I was confused. It came from behind me, and I didn't see the flash."

Mr. Hicks smiled, as did the judge, but there was no boisterous laughter. For a moment, the growing tension between Price and Burchard was put on hold.

In a bold move, Burchard shifted to another matter. "I request that the court reconsider allowing Mr. Dick to testify as to the outstanding warrant against Patrick Hoffman."

The judge removed her glasses and looked at the prosecutor. "No. The ruling stands."

Little new information was revealed in Dick's subsequent testimony, and the witness was excused. John Dick felt temporary relief. Memories of his failure to rescue his friend and cohort had been painful.

Chapter 21

Weapons

The remaining testimony of state witnesses was lengthy and technically challenging to follow. It also left open what firearm had been used on victims. The defense attacked the premise that FBI analyses proved that the bullet removed from Millard was fired from the K-99 9-millimeter, or that the slug removed from McGinnis was fired from John Dick's revolver. Testy attorney exchanges continued. Objections over leading questions, improper foundations, and credentials of experts increased.

The absence of the alleged smoking gun and Francis Peoples's equivocal testimony over what Elmer may have said at Armstrong Meadows exposed weaknesses in the state's case. FBI forensic evidence did not entirely rule out the possibility that tribal officers other than Millard and Dick had fired shots toward the chicken coop.

Officers on the scene were frightened if not terrified by the weapon reports. Officers Carden, Clark, Whitney, and Cox testified that they hunkered down when gunfire broke out, and thereafter retreated to their police cars. Chester Clark removed his shotgun from his car and took cover in a ditch. The others said they never drew their weapons during the melee.

Burchard called Robert Sivert, special agent for the FBI, to the stand. Agent Sivert recited his background: a degree in engineering and graduate work in forensic science. Sivert had served as a specialist in firearms identification for sixteen years.

"How would you describe your job as a firearms specialist?" asked Hicks.

"Firearms identification is the study of microscopic markings on fired ammunition components, bullets, and casings. These markings are then compared to the characteristics of a particular firearm to determine whether the weapon fired a given round," Sivert explained.

"What weapons did you examine?"

"I tested weapons from the gym bag and officers' service revolvers for firing characteristics. I also tested the 9-millimeter handgun found in Sergeant Millard's trunk."

Hicks wasted little time. He went to the most critical evidence of the trial. "Describe the bullet removed from Sergeant Millard."

"The bullet recovered from Sergeant Millard was a 9-millimeter, fully jacketed or full metal case bullet. This particular bullet showed rifling impressions indicating that it was fired from a barrel having six grooves with a right-hand twist," replied Sivert.

"What causes the grooves?"

"The grooves are caused when a slightly oversized bullet, such as from a 9-millimeter Luger cartridge, is forced down the barrel."

"Did investigators find Luger cartridges at the scene?"

"Yes. Two fired 9-millimeter Luger cartridges were found near a chicken cage near the back of the chicken coop."

"Did you examine these cartridges?"

"Yes. I first tested the casings to determine if the same weapon had fired them. Each firing pin leaves a microscopic fingerprint on the casing. I also examined breech face marks, marks left on the casing by the primer of a bullet. Based on these findings, I concluded the two casings were fired by the same firearm."

"What weapons could have been used to fire the bullet removed from Sergeant Millard?"

"The width, direction, and number of rifling grooves narrowed the weapons to seven known 9-millimeter firearms."

"Could you describe these weapons and the likelihood of any being the murder weapon?"

"One weapon that could have fired the removed bullet was an Interdynamics KG-99 nine-millimeter semiautomatic."

"What other weapons may have been used in the fatal shooting of Sergeant Millard?"

"Other weapons include handguns made by Browning, Luger, Radom, and Walther. The Mac-10, a semiautomatic or submachine gun, and a Volunteer Arms Commando rifle also may have been used," Sivert said.

"Did you find other evidence that narrowed the list of possible weapons?"

"Yes. Blowback action marks were present on the casings. A blowback feature is consistent with casings fired from an Interdynamics KG-99 firearm. By contrast, there was no evidence that these two cartridges were pivoted, and dropped down, and locked, such as found in guns with a recoil action."

"What about the quality of the KG-99?"

"They're one of the most dangerous firearms I am called upon to test in the laboratory," replied Sivert.

"I object," Price said, and requested a sidebar. "The testimony as to the dangerousness of the weapon is prejudicial. Such characterization could be construed to mean that anyone who owned such a weapon also would be considered dangerous."

Hicks explained, "Sometimes questions are unartfully asked. The thrust of Agent Sivert's statement was that this weapon is dangerous to test in a laboratory because it is subject to jamming. There was no attempt to say that this weapon is more dangerous than any other firearm."

The judge cut off debate. "The jury will be instructed to disregard Mr. Sivert's statement about dangerous firearms. The question should be rephrased to examine the risk of testing the weapon."

Burchard switched to another concern. "It's a minor thing," he explained. "We are having a slight problem with defendants handling exhibits during breaks."

Price said with apparent indignation, "To suggest that they can't handle it shocks me. I can't imagine why a deputy told Patrick to get his hands off the evidence. I let the deputy know that whoever was giving him those directions should talk to me and not to Mr. Hoffman. Prosecutors need to look at their own handling of evidence, where certain things in their evidence packets turn out to be something different." Price was referring to the FBI's miscount of cartridges delivered to defense forensic expert Ray Davis on February 10.

Trying to avoid another acrimonious exchange, Hicks said, "I am not going to respond to anything. The defendants were not doing anything wrong. But it would be of benefit if the clerk responsible for the evidence were present when the evidence is examined."

Judge Alumbaugh said firmly, "Handling of evidence will be restricted to the defendants, their attorneys, and witnesses offering testimony." She remarked to Deputy Clerk Patsy, "The clerk will always be present when evidence is examined, and evidence will be returned to the clerk without any unauthorized observer covertly or overtly having access."

Agent Sivert continued his testimony the next morning, Friday the thirteenth. He clarified his earlier remark about the danger of testing an Interdynamics KG-99 firearm. "On occasion, the bolt does not move fully forward. This can cause the case to rupture when fired, and pieces of brass are thrown from the ejection port, endangering the shooter." Sivert added, "The KG-99 is subject to jamming more than higher quality firearms."

"Was the bullet taken from Louis Millard consistent with the grooving found on an Interdynamics KG-99 firearm?" asked Hicks.

"Yes, sir, it is," replied Sivert.

Richard Price objected. "Agent Sivert's response misstates his previous testimony that there were seven firearms consistent with that grooving." The objection was sustained.

In response, Prosecutor Hicks rephrased his question. "Could other weapons have fired the lethal bullet?"

"Yes."

"Did you examine the groove patterns of tribal police weapons at the scene?"

"Yes. I first checked the caliber of the weapons and their respective cartridges. Weapons from Officers Phillips, Clark, Carden, Millard, and Dick were identified as .357 Magnum Smith & Wesson firearms."

"Was there any evidence that these firearms could have fired the 9-millimeter bullet removed from Sergeant Millard?"

"None of those firearms could have fired the 9-millimeter bullet. That bullet was fired from a barrel with six grooves, right twist, unlike the pattern from the Smith & Wesson .357."

"Did you examine the 9-millimeter semiautomatic that belonged to Vicki Ross?"

"I examined this handgun and determined that it was rifled with five grooves, right-hand twist, unlike the bullet in question with six grooves, right twist."

"Of all the weapons sent to your laboratory, could any have fired the fatal bullet?"

"None of the weapons sent to the lab could have fired the fatal bullet."

Hicks directed Agent Sivert to the bullet removed from Elmer McGinnis and asked, "What weapons could be linked to this projectile?"

"I concluded that the removed bullet was from a .38-caliber jacketed hollow-point cartridge like those manufactured by Winchester Western. It can be fired from a .357 since the difference in circumference is minimal—thousandths of an inch. It was very difficult to get a firm diameter reading on this projectile due to its mutilated condition. The rifling impression indicated the bullet was fired from a gun with five grooves and a right-hand twist. This was the same rifling pattern of the Smith & Wesson revolvers from Officers Phillips, Clark, Carden, Millard, and Dick. However, I could not conclude which revolver fired the bullet."

"What did you find out from cartridges sent to the laboratory?"

"When checking cartridges and casings found at the scene, I concluded that the ammunition used by Officers Dick and Carden matched the bullet removed from Elmer McGinnis—Winchester Western .38 caliber hollow-point ammunition. Hollow points have a cavity in the middle of the bullet to expand as it impacts its target. This provides greater transfer of energy and reduces the risk of hitting secondary targets."

Sivert continued, "I reexamined the police weapons and determined that the bullet removed from Elmer McGinnis was not from Officer Millard's firearm. Sergeant Millard fired twice. The two fired cartridge casings were from a different manufacturer—CCI rather than Winchester Western. Officer Dick's revolver had one unfired cartridge in the cylinder of the revolver. This cartridge had the same observable characteristics of the bullet removed from McGinnis, and matched eighteen other cartridges found in Officer Dick's speed loader. However, cartridges from Officer Carden's revolver also had the same characteristics."

"What was the source of the bullet found in a field adjacent to the McGinnis property?" Hicks asked.

"I was in a query as to the exact source of that bullet. I found the weight to be 113.6 grains. If it was a 9-millimeter bullet, somehow 1.4 grains were lost. The characteristics of the bullet were consistent with a 9-millimeter cartridge."

"That's all for the moment," Hicks said.

Price opened his cross-examination by attacking the expert's conclusions. "Out of all of this testimony, the one association that's conclusive in your study is that Mr. McGinnis was shot by a bullet from either Mr. Millard's, Mr. Carden's, or Mr. Dick's weapon. Is that correct?"

"No, that is not correct," replied Sivert.

"Yet you just testified that each of these weapons was associated with characteristics of the bullet from Mr. McGinnis. Is that not correct?"

"Yes, I made mention of a lot of associations. I am saying that the rifling impressions are compatible with any of the law enforcement revolvers here, but the cartridge cases from Mr. Dick's revolver were consistent with this bullet's manufacturer. They were different from those in Mr. Millard's revolver."

"But you cannot eliminate other weapons as potential sources of the bullet. Is this not correct? All you have is associative evidence. Is this not correct?"

"I agree that what I found is the best associative evidence we have available. On that basis, the most consistent evidence indicates that the bullet removed from McGinnis was fired from Mr. Dick's weapon."

"Well, associative evidence does not mean proof of which weapon fired the bullet that hit Mr. McGinnis, right?"

"Associative evidence is not proof of which weapon fired the bullet that hit Elmer McGinnis."

Burchard and Hicks finalized their argument that the defendants had purchased the alleged murder weapon, an Interdynamics KG-99 9-millimeter pistol, a little over a year before the firefight with police. Kenneth H. Ramble, owner of Ramble's Sports Shop in Colville, confirmed the purchase of the weapon. The witness characterized Patrick as a regular buyer of guns over a period of twenty years, and saw him as a responsible sportsman.

Mr. Ramble was excused. The judge called for a recess and went to her desk in Judge Thomas's office to make notes in her diary. She clearly was displeased. Trial observers reacted loudly at times to exchanges between Price and Burchard. Throughout the trial, the judge had made clear her concern over courtroom decorum and, most important in her view, security.

As a precaution during pretrial, Judge Alumbaugh had requested that Sheriff Johnston set up a metal detector for those entering the courtroom. The judge was concerned about congestion at the only entrance to the courtroom. All were checked for weapons, even law enforcement officers attending the trial. A plainclothes officer assigned to provide security was the only armed individual in the courtroom.

Yet, something else was bothering the judge, beyond security and even the sometimes raucous reactions of court observers—frequent contact between the deputy county clerk, Patsy, and Patrick Hoffman.

Chapter 22

The State Rests

Prosecutors shifted focus for the remainder of the trial to the source and trajectory of bullets fired during the skirmish.

FBI Agent Jim Davis was called to the stand. His presence throughout the trial while serving as a case agent for the state could hardly be ignored. For Richard Price, the jurors' exposure to the many appearances of an FBI agent seated near the prosecutor's table was a way of putting a thumb on the scales of justice. His familiarity and authoritative style as a witness could be sufficient to tilt the jury toward a guilty verdict in a case where the evidence was largely circumstantial.

Agent Davis repeated testimony about the location of weapons and shell casings, and went into some detail about his investigation of bullet trajectories. Two-by-fours and plywood sections from the scene were arranged on a table.

Hicks directed the agent to elaborate on the size, fragment, and penetration patterns of bullet holes in a plywood section from the south end of the chicken coop. Agent Davis described how, on September 4, 1986, he performed an on-site investigation of the trajectory of bullets fired during the fracas. A long, straight rod was inserted into the bullet holes found in the chicken coop and the fence post. The entry hole for the fence post was on the smooth side facing the chicken coop, while the fragmentation of the post was to the east. Based on the direction of the rod inserted into the fence post, Davis concluded that the bullet was fired from the chicken coop toward the place where Sergeant Millard dropped his flashlight.

Hicks exhibited photographs of the crime scene to the jury, including the chicken coop, chicken boxes behind the coop, flags to show the position of Sergeant Millard's flashlight and revolver, and the fence post as seen from along the east property line.

The prosecutor asked Davis about a set of photos overlooking the roof of the chicken coop. Davis described how BIA Agent Al Aubertin stood on a chicken box near the back of the coop and directed his camera toward Davis, who stood near a flag marking where Sergeant Millard had dropped his flashlight. The photo exposed Davis's profile from the waist up. Another photo, with Davis atop the box and Aubertin near the flag, showed Davis pointing his finger as though firing a gun toward Agent Aubertin.

The inference was clear. One of the defendants had climbed onto the chicken box to monitor officer movement. After the first shot was fired, one defendant, most likely Patrick, fired the K-99 at Sergeant Millard from that position. Given Elmer McGinnis's fatigue and poor health, it seemed unlikely that he would have climbed on the chicken box.

The state wrapped up their case by calling Jeffrey Epperson to the stand. "Do you have any personal knowledge about the guns that Patrick Hoffman owned?" asked Burchard.

"I've done some target practice with Pat. Usually Pat keeps his weapons in a gym bag in the seat next to him in his car."

"What types of guns did Patrick carry in his bag?"

"He usually carried three types: a .45, a 9-millimeter, and a .22. Usually we did our shooting at the rodeo grounds behind my house, and sometimes at Silver Creek. The .45 was like a military Colt .45, although Pat told me it was an Italian .45."

"What about the 9-millimeter?"

"It was a tube-fed semiautomatic. It was about, oh, eighteen, twenty inches long. Had a pistol grip with a magazine that came in the bottom. It had two magazines, one taped to the end of the other one, or side by side, you know, taped around her. To operate the gun, you just put the clip in the bottom and pull the bolt back and let her fire…just pull the trigger and she shot."

"How many rounds did the magazines hold?"

"I think each clip held twenty-six and thirty rounds, for a total of fifty-six rounds. That was what Pat and I talked about. Yeah, that's right."

"When Patrick appeared at your door, how did he look?" Burchard asked.

"He was plum scared. He was looking for a partner. Pat was dressed in Levi's with cowboy boots and a coat tied around his waist. I asked him if he had any weapons with him. He said no. I said, 'Come on in,' you know. And that's when he was saying that his dad had been shot and killed, and he just wanted to get out. He was afraid he was going to get killed. He was really scared. I told him that Elmer wasn't killed, that he had been shot and he was in the hospital. That's when I told him Lou Millard had been shot and killed."

"What was Patrick's reaction?"

"He said 'good deal' that—"

"In regard to the officer or Elmer McGinnis?"

"I object, Your Honor. I insist that the witness have a chance to finish his answer to the previous question," Price said.

"Sure," answered Burchard. "Is there something you want to add to that?"

"Well, he was, you know, really shook up. And like I say, he was concerned about his dad, and I told him about that and he calmed down. And then I told him about Lou Millard being killed and he said, 'Good deal,' you know."

"Was Patrick responding to being told that his dad was alive or that Lou Millard was dead?"

"I think it was about Mr. Millard being dead."

Chapter 23

Rooftop Dispute

Richard Price called Raymond Davis as a witness for defendant Hoffman. The forensic scientist was retained by the defense to examine physical evidence the FBI gathered at the McGinnis residence and provide an assessment of his visit to the scene.

"What is your background in forensic science?"

"After graduating from California State University in 1972 with a degree in chemistry, I was hired by the California Department of Justice as a criminalist. I spent seven years analyzing physical evidence for law enforcement agencies. I took special courses in firearms examination, body wounds, and crime scene reconstruction. Also, I trained law enforcement officers on how to collect evidence."

The forensic expert's testimony was lengthy and, like Special Agent Sivert's testimony, at times replete with unfamiliar ballistic references. Price focused on whether any conclusions could be reached as to what gun fired what bullet.

Regarding the bullet removed from Sergeant Millard, Davis testified, "While the round has visible land and groove width measurements, there is no way to narrow down the field of potential 9-millimeter weapons. Such measurements would not help much, given there are literally hundreds of thousands of weapons that could have fired these rounds. There's no way to tell if they had been ejected from a gun fired in a burst or at different times." Davis said that the casings found behind the chicken coop were not matched to any weapon. "I could find no evidence of when they were fired or by whom."

Davis also examined Officer Millard's chest protector and shirt. He concluded that the bullet entered at the V-shaped gap above the protector.

Comparing the bullet from Elmer McGinnis to the weapons presented to him, Raymond Davis concluded that the bullet came either from Officer Dick's or Officer Carden's revolver. Officer Millard's gun was eliminated because that night he was using a Winchester Western 145-grain, silver-tip, semi-jacketed round, which did not match up with the McGinnis bullet.

Price asked Davis to assess the testimony of FBI Agent Jim Davis as to photos taken at the scene. Price asked what someone standing on a chicken box could have seen over the rooftop, looking toward Sergeant Millard's flashlight.

Hicks objected and requested a sidebar. A lengthy debate erupted over whether Raymond Davis could testify on the matter.

Hicks reacted strongly. "The expert can only testify as to what could not have happened. What scientific certainty does he offer? Basically, he's giving his opinion, which is really no different than asking a defense attorney or a prosecutor to reconstruct the scene based on their individual experience in handling criminal cases. He wasn't there that night."

"Agent Davis certainly wasn't there that night, and that was the first time we'd ever heard of standing on a box," Price said.

"He didn't testify to that. He testified that he could get up on the box and see somebody from the waist up, for whatever value that is," Judge Alumbaugh reminded counsel.

"He was asked to hold his hand up and point in the direction of a gun, and he did," Price shot back.

While the sidebar was intended to be outside the jury's hearing range, the judge worried that the raised voices could be heard. She asked that the jury be removed. Price saw this as an opportune time to offer new evidence. "I have a videotape I would like the court to review while the jury is out."

"A tape? When did this come up?" Burchard said.

"Sunday," answered Price, "when your expert got up on the stand and said that he stood on those boxes—the first time we ever heard about it in the six months of this trial."

"Well, you never interviewed him," the prosecutor said.

The judge decided to excuse the jury for a break, and return for a private viewing of the tape. Mr. Gardner set the stage for when and how the video was produced the previous weekend, on Sunday, March 22. "Richard Price, Bill Cottrell, Joe Larkin, and I gathered at the southeast corner of the chicken coop. We set out to demonstrate the view from the chicken coop rooftop looking directly toward Sergeant Millard's flashlight and Officer Dick's speed loader. You will see that, from that position, there was no clear view of the officers," Gardner said. "Richard Price took a position at the approximate location of Officer Millard's flashlight. I repositioned a chicken crate to the spot indicated by Sergeant Carden's photographs. I then climbed onto the crate and shot a video from over the chicken coop looking toward Richard Price."

After showing the tape, Price proposed that Ray Davis testify as to whether the video represented the area he saw on his visit to the property. "Also, I will ask his opinion as to whether a person firing on top of the chicken boxes could cause the bullet wound on the long axis of Mr. Millard's body, assuming he was standing in the area identified by the state."

Burchard objected. "This expert is not qualified to talk about the angle of the bullet into a person. He is basically doing crime scene reconstruction, which is not accepted expert testimony." As to the tape, Mr. Burchard said, with some skepticism, "There are several questions. How accurate was Mr. Price's position, his height, and what boxes were positioned from where, and proximity to their original positions? Making attorneys witnesses introduces other issues. Mr. Davis doesn't know anything about where the boxes were on August twenty-seventh, and can hardly comment on the appropriateness of the experiment since he wasn't there."

Price said he wanted to preserve his right to make a closing argument by having the court accept the foundation for the tape without the jury present. "I'll ask Ray Davis his opinion as to whether somebody firing from that position would be consistent with a bullet striking Mr. Millard and taking the path it did through his body," he explained to the judge.

"In a word, no. No. It doesn't hold together, counsel, that this man can come in and see a videotape that somebody else put together, and is now going to use that as a basis for his expert opinion on anything," challenged the judge.

Price took exception, saying the tape was not the basis for his opinion. Rather, "Ray Davis visited the scene and read Dr. Bonifaci's report. We thought the tape would be of assistance to the jury, to see the scene and have it depicted on film."

Judge Alumbaugh would not yield. "Well, you can't use the tape with this witness."

Price pressed for a second portion of the defense's argument. "We want to elicit Mr. Davis's opinion as to whether a wound described in Dr. Bonifaci's report is consistent with a person firing a gun from atop cages behind the chicken coop."

"You're going to have to make an offer of proof that sets up more background or expertise than what you have so far, counsel, because I don't see any basis for this man making that particular statement," charged the judge.

"I prefer offering a foundation in front of the jury," Price responded.

"So that I can send them out again if need be?"

"The witness will comment on the lay of the land, including the height and position of the chicken coop in front of the cages."

"The witness is not qualified with his background to comment on the path of the bullet. He's not a pathologist," replied the judge.

"The target of the question is a human body. Agent Sivert, who has expertise in analyzing bullet trajectories, said he could not offer an opinion when a bullet hits a human body," Burchard challenged. "Such analyses should be left to a forensic pathologist."

Price, perhaps sensing that there was no point in going any further with the "long-axis" inquiry, offered, "I will limit my questions to how the energy of a bullet fired from a forty-five-degree angle atop the chicken coop would enter and travel through an object standing at a ninety-degree angle. No questions on pathology will be asked."

"So, you're going to have this man get up and testify that when you pull a trigger, the bullet goes in the direction the barrel is pointed?" asked the judge derisively.

"The law of physics, Your Honor: for every action there's a reaction," answered Price with some aplomb.

"Do you think that takes an expert, Mr. Price, or ordinary common sense?"

Price answered, "This is the most appropriate witness to answer such questions."

"Your witness can testify as to his own observations, but not his opinion about state reports concerning someone firing at a target over the chicken coop from atop chicken boxes."

Price relentlessly insisted that the defense have an opportunity to show the other side of the state's case. "Our expert is more qualified than Agent Jim Davis in terms of forensic science. He can determine whether the evidence is consistent with that scenario."

Burchard interjected, "Can I ask Ray Davis if he ever stood on those chicken cages?"

Davis answered without objection, "I never stood on them, but stood behind the chicken coop."

"This is why the tape is necessary. Ray Davis needs to tell jurors his conditional theory of the case, if someone were standing on the box and viewing from that angle toward Officer Millard's flashlight," Price replied.

"Mr. Davis did not perform the test himself. He did not stand on any of the chicken boxes and look over the chicken coop. And, Mr. Davis cannot testify in an in area where he has little background, forensic pathology. The ruling stands. Mr. Davis cannot comment on the angle of the shot directed at Officer Millard," the judge insisted.

The jury was called back.

Price continued his examination. "Those casings—if they were actually located there at the time of the shooting, would that be consistent with a person standing on top of the chicken cages and firing from that position?"

"As they're shooting forward, no, because semiautomatic weapons tend to eject their rounds up and to the right rear," Davis said. "Ejection can vary from five to fifteen feet, depending on the cycle of fire and the condition of the weapon."

"Based on your on-site visit, what did you observe?" Price asked.

"I positioned myself behind the chicken coop in various locations, with my associate standing at the site where Lou Millard's flashlight was found. I could not see her from behind the coop."

Price repeated the expert's previous testimony. "Regarding the location of the 9-millimeter casings found near a chicken cage, is their location consistent with a person standing on top of the chicken cages and firing from that position?"

"As they're shooting forward, no," Davis said. "That would apply to targets to the north and northeast." He repeated his rationale based on the expected ejection of rounds from a 9-millimeter semiautomatic weapon. Davis concluded that the only associative evidence from all the physical evidence he examined was that the round taken from Mr. McGinnis could have been fired from Dick's or Carden's weapon.

The defense called to the stand Sheila Cleveland, Elmer's neighbor to the north of Cache Creek Road. She recounted how Officer Clark took cover in a ditch. Cleveland testified that she invited him in the house to treat what Clark alleged was a gunshot wound. Clark remained in the house until well after the shooting had ceased.

As a follow-up to Cleveland's testimony, Price called Officer Clark to the stand and explored what happened when he first arrived and later when he received aid from Cleveland. Clark testified that he grabbed his shotgun and took cover when he heard a shot fired; he never fired his weapon. He remained in that position until a flare appeared to be shot at him, and at that point he retreated.

Price skillfully exposed the officer's misadventures with his weapons. According to testimony, he lost his revolver once under his police vehicle, and again on the road while running for cover. His thumb wound was actually from striking his shotgun when he took cover in a ditch after hearing a bevy of shots.

The defense laid the groundwork to question police protocol before, during, and after the gun battle, but was the jury convinced that police negligently caused the outbreak, or in fact fired the fatal bullet? Price had pressed John Dick about telling the doctor he had been hit in his chest, not his back. If true, did Lou Millard actually fire a shot toward the chicken coop, hitting John Dick instead of Elmer McGinnis?

The absence of the KG-99 was problematic for both sides. The missing weapon meant that Sivert could not narrow the smoking gun to only the KG-99. Raymond Davis found no basis to conclude that any weapon could be linked to the bullet removed from Sergeant Millard. Direct examination of the missing weapon would settle the issue. If experts had determined the 9-millimeter was not the source of the lethal bullet, first-degree murder charges most likely would not have been filed in the first place.

Chapter 24

Patrick Hoffman Takes the Stand

Patrick and Elmer grew more impatient with the way the trial was progressing. Patrick told his attorney that Burchard had distorted his involvement. Elmer continued to complain that corrupt officials had not been exposed. This is why the shooting took place. It was simple. Tribal police resorted to overwhelming force to take him out for what he knew.

Patrick pressed Price to correct the record. He wanted to testify. He felt confident that he could convince the jury he was caring for his father as they made their way home over backcountry. Once there, he had no choice but to defend his father when attacked by unknown invaders.

Price warned Patrick of the pitfalls of taking the stand. Prosecutors could ask him directly about his intent in carrying an arsenal of weapons to the scene. Patrick would be pressed on what weapons he had fired and at whom. His statement to Jeff Epperson, that Elmer had fired the K-99, might be allowed.

Patrick listened to his attorney, but he felt confident that he could answer such questions and clarify what really happened. He felt strongly that most of the damaging testimony had been taken out of context.

Price had no choice if his client insisted. Patrick had a constitutional right to testify, but Price asked him to consider another option—a "lesser included" instruction that would allow the jury to consider a lesser charge, such as second-degree murder, if they could not agree on the charge of aggravated first-degree murder. Bud Gardner made the same offer to Elmer.

Price advised Patrick to seriously consider accepting the state's offer for the lesser included instruction. He spelled out the benefits of doing significantly less time if the jury found evidence lacking for the aggravated murder charge but would agree to a lesser charge. The state's case was built on circumstantial evidence. The jury could hang on the "beyond reasonable doubt" standard as to who fired the fatal shot. Price highlighted other evidentiary problems. Patrick listened, but refused to agree to the instruction.

Elmer was even more forceful on the matter. "Goddamnit, we are innocent, period. There is no way I am about to admit guilt in any degree," he said. "Why should we admit to a crime we did not do?"

On Friday morning, March 20, the defense announced each client's refusal to accept the lesser included instruction. "It is your right to turn down the instruction," the judge said. She spelled out the ramifications of the special instruction and proffered, "I want both of you to reconsider your decision with your attorneys and sleep on the matter. I will ask you again of your decision when we return on Monday."

After a weekend of thought and, on occasion, stormy consultation with their clients, Price and Gardner announced to the judge that both clients still refused the lesser instruction. "Do you understand that the jury will not be instructed to consider a lesser charge in their decision?" the judge asked. Both defendants said yes. The remainder of the day and Tuesday were consumed by debates over motions for the jury to visit the scene, a discussion of transportation logistics, and settling on a date.

Before calling his client to the stand on a bright Wednesday morning, Price requested that the jury be removed. He once again motioned to suppress evidence of a Ferry County arrest warrant for Patrick. "If Patrick Hoffman testifies, his arrest record could come into play," Price said. "I would like an understanding from the court before Patrick takes the stand that the misdemeanor assault conviction will be excluded."

Burchard rebutted, "If Mr. Hoffman takes the stand, the state fully intends to examine his state of mind as to why he thought officers were looking for him and his father. While Mr. Hoffman's past does not prove he's guilty of the underlying offense in this instance, his history is highly probative as to what Patrick Hoffman was thinking in the car and later during the shoot-out. Police were prevented from testifying that they knew of the arrest warrant and intended to execute the warrant that night."

"Police were not looking for anybody other than Mr. McGinnis. Mr. Hoffman was in the area for six months, and was not attempting to elude police, who did nothing to bring about an arrest during that period," Price argued.

Judge Alumbaugh grew impatient. "I will listen carefully to Mr. Hoffman's testimony and determine at that time what may or may not come in," she ruled. "I will not second-guess Mr. Hoffman's testimony by making a ruling in advance."

Price took exception. "This places my client in jeopardy if you make an unfavorable ruling on the matter of the arrest warrant."

"Would you like to discuss this with Mr. Hoffman before taking the stand?" the judge asked.

"Yes, I would," replied Price.

The judge took leave of the bench and returned after a lengthy break. She asked the jury to be seated. "Will the defense call its next witness?" she announced.

Mr. Price called Patrick Hoffman to the stand. "Could you identify yourself for the record?"

"I am Patrick Hoffman."

"What is your age and where do you presently reside?"

"I'm thirty-eight years old, and I reside at the Okanogan County Jail."

"Where is your permanent residence?"

"Keller, Washington."

"Have you lived there all your life?"

"No. I grew up in Inchelium with my parents, Clarence and Helen Hoffman. I had two brothers and six sisters, and I was the youngest of that family."

"How did you discover your natural father, Elmer McGinnis?"

"I discovered at age fourteen that my natural father was Elmer McGinnis. The Hoffman family and I had contact with Elmer, but it wasn't until my adopted father, Clarence, suffered a heart attack and had to retire early that I discovered my biological father. It came out when Clarence was filling out social security forms. Hearing this, I felt kind of a shock. It was something new that I had to adjust to. I had mixed feelings, and maybe some resentment for a while, but as time grew and I grew, I learned to accept Elmer. I did visit the family after that, but I never lived with him.

"About the time that Clarence suffered a heart attack, I also discovered who my natural mother was. I served as an altar boy with the Catholic Church, and I had participated in a service for last rites to an individual who someone later told me was my mother. I discussed it with the Hoffmans, about where I was going to reside, and I decided that I would go ahead and apply for my adoption into the Hoffman family," Patrick elaborated. Patrick elaborated he had not been formally adopted during his early childhood. Signing up as a dependent qualified Clarence Hoffman for Social Security benefits.

Given his vocal and instrumental talents, Patrick was awarded a music scholarship to Central Washington University, where he met Marion Page, a music major, and courted her. The couple married and celebrated the birth of their son, Robert Patrick. The marriage faltered, and Patrick took up a nomadic life in California. He returned to the reservation. Going back to his roots in music, Patrick formed a band that had marginal success. After years of playing small venues, the band seemed to jell between 1982 and 1986.

"Did you make further contact with Elmer upon returning to the reservation?" Price asked.

"Over the years the contact with my father increased. We got together for dinners at my sisters' houses in Keller. I got to know him as my father."

"In recent years, did you discuss concerns he may have had with the tribal council and police?"

"He showed me documents that he saw as evidence of these misdeeds. It was basically my dad's concern. For me, it was only in passing. I was aware of the possibility that things were not what they appeared to be, but I really didn't get into it that much."

"Do you own a gym bag and carry your gym bag with you most times?"

"Yes. I did have weapons and carried the bag with me because that's the way I was reared. The Hoffmans taught me how to handle firearms and appreciate their intended use. Marie, elder daughter of the Hoffmans, taught me to shoot when I was quite young."

"Are you an active game hunter?"

"Clarence took me hunting at age twelve, and I shot my first deer. Since then, I have owned firearms most of my life. So yes, I enjoy hunting," replied Patrick.

"Did you collect firearms?"

"Firearms are more or less a hobby for me. During 1985, I owned a .45, a .22 pistol, several hunting rifles, a .25-20, a .25-06, and things of that nature. I also owned a .303 British rifle from World War II. I liked to go out and target practice. The .22 pistol was a gift from my dad to me and my sister, Fran. It was an antique and had value as such. He'd given various firearms to other family members as an expression of his gratitude and love of his family."

"What was your relationship with Mr. Ramble?"

"He was a family friend. My father and I traveled to Colville to special order a 9-millimeter semiautomatic. This was not unusual. I had ordered other guns like the .25-06 and a Colt .22. I traded guns from time to time with friends. After six to eight weeks, the gun was shipped," answered Hoffman.

"On the night of August 26, what firearms did you have in your gym bag?"

"I had three firearms in my bag: a .22, a .45, and a 9-millimeter."

"Did you carry the bag frequently?"

"I used the bag to organize various things for travel such as my music. I could put it on the back of my motorcycle, and I did so to maintain the safety of my firearms and pack things like clothing for myself and others riding with me. I traveled with the bag most times."

"Did you carry firearms in your bag because Elmer told you that there was a contract out on each of you?"

"He did tell me that there was a contract out on myself and him. At the time, I thought it was odd, but it really didn't register as something to be concerned about. Later while I was playing at a tavern, a gentleman came up to me and expressed that same statement."

"Who did you believe put out such a contract?"

"I knew Bobby Jo Covington. I was somewhat aware of his concerns about the tribal council. Bobby wanted tribal reform where members could express their opinions, where reservation issues were put to the people from time to time rather than the council making all these decisions. I was aware that he died in an accident in 1982."

Price produced exhibit thirteen, a .22 pistol, and exhibit fourteen, a .45 handgun. "Do you recognize these guns?"

"Yes, these are my weapons."

Price shifted to Elmer's hospitalization and discharge. "What did Dr. Justus tell you and your family concerning Elmer's hospitalization?"

"The doctor said that he could go home as long as he had somebody there to help take care of him. He gave us some instructions on a breathing exercise to prevent pneumonia."

"What did you do next?"

"I drove the car up to the front door of the hospital. No one told us that Dad was under arrest or that there was a hold on him. A nurse came up to Dad and took him by the arm and asked if he needed a wheelchair or some help. Lila was talking to a nurse, and Dad turned to her and said, 'Come on, we're wasting time; let's go.'"

"What was your destination?"

"To get Dad back home for rest and to take care of the animals. We headed for the Pass."

"I assume you mean Disautel Pass—Highway 155?"

"Yes."

"What did you observe while traveling on Highway 155?"

"I saw a police vehicle approach as we were about over the summit of the small pass. My father was alarmed when he saw the police car make a U-turn behind us. He appeared to be in pursuit."

"How did you respond?"

"I asked if there was a road to turn off on, and one of the girls said there was one up ahead. I may have sped up to get to that road. It was a dirt road that put up a lot of dust when we traveled over it. I did not see any police vehicle with any flashing lights or siren behind me."

"How far did you travel on that road?"

"I traveled about a mile or something like that. My dad said that he wanted out, so I stopped the car. It was near dusk. He was afraid that the police were trying to get him, and he was concerned about the girls' safety. We were concerned about him and his welfare."

"What happened next?"

"I got out about the same time dad did. I was determined that my father was not about to go anywhere on foot in his condition without me. I got my gym bag and a flare kit that was in the back of Lila's vehicle. I figured if some-thing went wrong with my father where I had to contact somebody, where I needed to inform somebody of our location, I would use it."

"Was there any plan to set up an ambush on tribal police?"

"There was never any plan by anyone, including my father, to set up an ambush or to kill tribal policemen. My only concern was to make sure Dad was safe. That's why I went along with him. He just wanted to get home, to not have any contact with police officers or anybody else. There was no way I would leave my father. Dad was in no condition to make it home over rough terrain for that distance—maybe fifteen miles."

"What happened after you exited the car?"

"I wasn't sure at all that my father was capable of walking home. He had heart problems, and he had just been taken off a heart monitor. We'd walk awhile and then we'd rest. He was having a lot of difficulty." Patrick said they stopped two times, and he implored Elmer to call it a night or seek shelter with a nearby neighbor. Elmer refused. "I figured we traveled six miles, maybe more. I had never been in the area on foot before. We reached a hill above my father's residence just behind the HUD houses on the northeast end of town. After a rest, we walked down Cache Creek Road toward the house. We walked under a streetlight, crossed the highway, and went up the driveway to the house. Then we realized that we didn't have the key. Laura had it."

"Tell us what happened next."

"I could see lights coming up toward the house. They stopped some-where down the driveway. I was concerned, and Dad said, 'Let's go back up behind the chicken coop.' From behind the coop we saw another set of lights east of the house. This seemed odd to me at the time. We were intent on stay-ing behind the coop to avoid being seen until we figured out who was there."

"Was there any way you could determine who was shining the lights toward you?"

"We didn't know who might be down there. We had tried to avoid con-tact with police that night on our way home. That's why we got out of the car in the first place."

"Where were you located precisely behind the chicken coop?"

"At one point we went to the east end of the coop, and I set down my bag. There were lights on the property, and the only place that was dark was directly behind the chicken coop. I felt closed in, and I opened the bag and took out my .22 and the .45. I told Dad, 'Let's stay concealed. Maybe they'll go away if we aren't seen or anything,'" Patrick explained.

"Did you reposition yourself then?"

"Yeah, I went back to the west end of the coop, and I remained there. The lights still shone on the hills behind us. On the east side, the lights went dim or went out, I'm not sure. Anyway, right after that there was firing and a lot of things broke loose."

"Did you hear any verbal warnings or shouts prior to hearing gun shots?"

"I didn't hear any noise before the shooting broke out. I didn't hear anything other than just all of a sudden there were gunshots coming from behind me."

"What happened next?"

"I turned around and saw my father, saw his silhouette going down. He was heading toward the back of the chicken coop. Somebody was shooting at us. I took the .22 and I shot over the building into the air to either draw fire or repel whoever was shooting at us. I fired about eight rounds," replied Hoffman. "I was able to make it over to my father at the southeast corner of the coop. He was on the ground when he told me, 'I'm hit.' I asked where, and he said his chest. There was a lot of blood. The bag was right there near him. I got a handkerchief out and tried to stop the bleeding."

"Describe what happened next."

"All of a sudden there were more shots coming at me, so I took my .45 and returned fire. I emptied the clip. I didn't know who I was firing at. All I saw as I looked around the edge of the building were muzzle flashes, and I fired in that general direction."

"Did you or Elmer fire any flares?"

"Somewhere along in there I put some flares in the air. I believe my father fired some flares. The flares started a fire. By then the shooting had more or less died down and it was quiet again. There was smoke coming up between the lights, and I said to Dad, 'Let's get out of here. We've got to get you some help.' I helped him up. We started up behind the chicken coop. I had to lift Dad up over both fences, and we started up over the hill," Hoffman replied.

"What happened to the 9-millimeter pistol?"

"At various times he or I or both of us had a hold of that weapon. I also had my .45 in my holster when we headed up the hill. The hill got very steep, and my dad was having trouble. Somewhere back there he went down, and I picked him up and put him on my back. At that point I wasn't concerned about the weapons; I was just trying to get him out of there."

"Describe what happened next."

"We got to a grove of trees, to a flat area. We had no weapons. There were still lights shining up on the hillside just below us. Smoke was still coming across the area. I figured we could not be seen because we cast no shadows. My father asked me to put him down. He said he had to lie down and rest. He told me he couldn't go any farther, and he said, 'I'm done for.' He told me to get out of there before they killed me, too. I left. At the time, I didn't have any weapons with me. I went over the top of the hill."

"What was your destination?"

"Through the following day and the next night and most of the day after that, I headed for Keller. I didn't know what I was going to do. I was very, very scared," Patrick said. "It was tough going. The terrain was steep. I got to the ridge and over it. I thought along the way about my father's condition when I left him, and concluded that he was dead. His wound was pretty bad. I finally arrived at Jeff Epperson's place the following afternoon."

"What is your relationship with Jeffrey Epperson?"

"Jeff has been a friend of mine for the last two or three years."

"Describe what happened after you arrived at the Epperson house."

"I knocked on the back door, and a small boy appeared. After a short time, Jeff came to the door. We talked about what should be done. I learned that my father had not been killed. Jeff also told me that an officer had been killed that night. He showed me a newspaper."

"How did you respond to the news?"

"As to Jeff testifying that I said, 'Good deal,' I was feeling relieved that my father was alive—that's what I was feeling," replied Hoffman. "I was not responding to the downed officer."

"What plans did you make after this disclosure?" asked Price.

"We talked about strategy. Jeff said the best course was to turn myself in to the FBI or county officials. After reading the newspaper article, I was very much concerned about my safety."

"What did you decide?"

"I agreed to make a call to the county sheriff, Johnny Johnston. I told the sheriff I wanted to turn myself in. Fred Leskinen, Jeff's neighbor, and me talked about the dangers of being seen in the pickup. Jeff and Fred put together a disguise with a hat, a bandanna, and sunglasses for me to wear to get past police at home."

"Tell us about your transfer from the Okanogan County Jail," Price said.

"Jim Davis, the FBI guy, picked me up and we flew to Spokane. On the flight, I may have said something like 'everything just seemed to erupt and I didn't think it would turn out that way,' but that did not mean in any way that I or my dad had a plan to attack police."

Price said, "That's all I have for now."

Gardner rose to cross-examine the defendant. "Did you observe Elmer McGinnis fire a weapon?"

"I heard some shots and turned around and saw my father falling. I never saw him fire a gun," Patrick said. "I didn't see him shoot a gun after that."

"Did you share your father's belief that the tribal council had a contract on you? If so, did you take these threats seriously?"

"At first I didn't take them seriously. I'm a musician. I play music. I don't—you know, it didn't have any relationship to me at the time."

"After seeing Elmer's documents regarding possible corruption, did you hold to the same opinion? Did you not take the threats seriously?"

"I looked at those documents and saw who was involved. I talked with others who had knowledge of those documents, and discovered that they had been handled by the tribal council. I thought there was a definite possibility of management corruption of one form or another."

Chapter 25

Cross-Examination

After Bud Gardner announced that he had no more questions, Jack Burchard had his chance to ask the defendant the tough questions that would have gone unanswered if Patrick had not taken the stand. What was Patrick's real motive to carry an arsenal of weapons, including flares, to the scene of the shoot-out? Who shot what weapon from what position? How would Patrick explain inconsistencies in his testimony, such as the remarks made to Jeff Epperson and Fred Leskinen?

Before the cross-examination, Judge Alumbaugh requested that the jury be removed. Patrick Hoffman was asked to step down. "Mr. Burchard, do you plan to introduce the arrest warrant from Ferry County?" the judge asked. "If so, the court needs some explanation as to how you intend to use it."

"We will argue that the warrant is admissible to show his motive, his state of mind, his premeditation, and his intent to kill," the prosecutor asserted. "His story is that he had no thought for anything except his father's welfare and his fear, and no knowledge of who might be pulling into the driveway with lights ablaze. The Ferry County arrest warrant establishes his state of mind. He was fleeing from the police. His testimony contradicted other witness accounts of what happened at the hospital."

"Based on testimony to date, there is no substantiation of the prosecutor's claims," Price argued. "Every police officer at the scene testified that police never identified themselves. Mr. Hoffman was not fleeing the police when he turned off the road and his father insisted on being let out of the car. There was no evidence that the bench warrant was motivating Mr. Hoffman that evening in any way. The bench warrant had been outstanding since February 1986. The police knew where Mr. Hoffman lived. He was not hiding. There were no attempts to execute this warrant."

"I have spent some time this morning reviewing previous testimony and looking at the case law on the matter," replied the judge. "I concluded that there was a danger of undue prejudice that outweighed the probative value if the warrant were introduced in cross-examination. I have to admit that I can't really see this relating directly to intent in terms of what happened that evening." The noise level from the packed courtroom made it difficult to hear, and the judge gaveled the court to order. "You on the back benches need to lower your voices. The court reporter is having difficulty hearing attorneys."

The noise subsided. The judge asked Patrick to step back on the stand. Burchard shuffled through his notes, rose, and approached the witness stand. "You have stated that you and your sisters were intent on taking your father home from the hospital. Was there a loud noise or anything else that would have prevented you from seeing the nurse, Sue Peterson, walk up to your father and grab him by the elbow?" asked the prosecutor.

"No, sir."

"And is it your testimony that she did not tell your father that he was on a police hold or under arrest, and that he was supposed to wait for the police?"

Price interjected, "Your Honor, I ask that the question be stricken as a mischaracterization of the evidence. Her testimony—"

"I demand a sidebar," Burchard interrupted.

At the bench, Burchard said, "I'm just trying to avoid speeches to the witness and to the jury. The court heard Ms. Peterson's testimony. This is cross-examination. It's not a mischaracterization."

"I understood her testimony to be that she informed him that he should wait because the police wanted to talk to him—nothing about a police hold or arrest," responded Price. Gardner agreed.

"That was not her testimony, Your Honor. She told Mr. McGinnis that the police would just look for him if he left," argued Burchard.

Price disagreed. "I don't recall that that was her testimony."

The debate drifted to interpretation of the Federal Rules of Evidence regarding misstatements or mischaracterizations of testimony, and the judge reached her tolerance limit. "Must we? I have heard enough. The prosecutor may ask about Nurse Peterson's statements as long as he does not characterize her testimony." Patrick returned to the stand.

"So, Mr. Hoffman, it's your testimony here today that Nurse Peterson didn't say anything to your father at all about the police?"

"Not that I heard, sir."

"She didn't tell him anything about a police hold?"

"I don't recall anything like that."

"Didn't she tell him that he might as well not leave because the police would come looking for him?"

"No, sir."

"When you encountered the police car on your drive from the hospital, had Elmer made statements about the police wanting to kill him?"

"Yes, sir."

"And you believed that?"

"Yes, sir."

"Based on what?"

"On his statements, sir."

"You didn't say to your father, 'Dad, calm down, nobody's going to get you. Let's go talk to the police and get this straightened out?'"

"I'm sorry. It's not my position to tell my dad what or what not to do. He's my father."

"So, whatever he says, you do?"

"I try to when it's within reason."

"Including shooting police officers?" the prosecutor challenged.

Richard Price leaped forward and strenuously objected. "The question must be stricken, and the jury be asked to disregard it. That's a mischaracterization of the testimony and it's prejudicial."

"It's no kind of mischaracterization, Your Honor. I think I can ask Mr. Hoffman if he killed police officers for his father," replied Burchard.

The judge removed the jury once again to settle the matter. "I move that we strike the question or declare a mistrial," Price insisted. The trial was winding down and Burchard and Price were reaching the boiling point yet again.

"The prosecutor has asked a question that is totally inconsistent with the answer of the witness, who stated that he would do what his father told him to do within reason. It was intended to do nothing but incite this jury—it's argumentative and prejudicial," Price chastised. "I consider it misconduct on Mr. Burchard's part, who seems a bit keyed up at this point. We have rung the bell once again because of the prosecutor's overzealousness in trying to paint a picture for which he has laid no foundation. Nobody indicated that he would kill anybody at the request of his father."

Burchard rebutted, "Well, I think I have a right to ask him about it, Your Honor. I think I have a right to test whether Mr. Hoffman really believed his father, and to find out just what he would do for his father. I have a right to challenge it, and I'm trying to do that in an appropriate way."

"What exactly are you asking of the court, Mr. Price?" the judge said.

"I am asking to strike the question and for the jury to disregard it, or the reverse."

"For a mistrial, Mr. Price?" asked the judge.

"Yes. I cannot think of a more prejudicial, argumentative statement after the witness had reasonably and conscientiously answered that he would try and do for his father what he considered reasonable," Price said.

"I think it's a legitimate question, Your Honor, within the fair bounds of a cross-examination," Burchard said. "There is evidence that the father and the son killed one police officer and shot another one in the back. I have a right to question him on their relationship, their planning, and on Mr. Hoffman's state of mind as to whether he does what his father tells him to do or not."

"I will not strike the question, but the prosecutor is advised to keep the questioning within bounds of good attorney practice," the judge said. "Let's not have any more interruptions, if possible, on this kind of argumentative questioning. The defense should be aware that this is cross-examination and there is some leeway."

Price persisted, "Are you going to allow counsel to propound that question and elicit an answer?"

"I am not going to insist that the prosecutor shift to another area," the judge replied. "After all, in a trial alleging aggravated first-degree murder, there are going to be some questions about whether or not this man participated in it. That's what he's on trial for."

Price consulted with Patrick about the ruling and its implications, then the judge brought the trial back to order. "Mr. Hoffman, please return to the witness stand."

Burchard shifted his cross-examination to Elmer's statement, when he exited the car, about concern for the girls' safety. Burchard then asked a series of questions about Elmer's alleged statements like "If those bastards come near me, I'm going to kill them." Patrick denied that any such comments were made. He also rejected the idea that he had any thoughts of getting even for the beating police had given Elmer the previous day.

The prosecutor then returned to the point where Patrick turned the Impala toward Armstrong Meadows. "At that point, you knew the police were after you?"

"I knew that they had turned around. I did not know that they were after us."

"You thought they were going after someone else—that's why you pulled on the dirt road?"

"That is a possibility, yes."

"And you don't even know if the police are looking for you, and you're going to let your father out six or eight miles from home to walk through the mountains?" asked the prosecutor cynically.

"I got out with him, sir, to help him. That was the best I could do."

"Isn't it true that the reason you didn't drive him to his house is because you knew the police were looking for you, and they were going to be waiting at the house when you got there?"

"No, sir, I didn't know that."

"The thought never crossed your mind?"

"No, sir."

"Oh, so your father was in the state that you've described—beat up, difficulty walking—and you were worried about his health, and so you got out to help him. Is that the idea basically?"

"Yes, sir."

"And you brought your gym bag along, as I understand from your testimony, because there was clothing in the bag. Is that all?"

"Yes, sir."

"Would you show the members of the jury—or tell us, excuse me—just what clothing was in the gym bag? Or maybe you can tell us if some clothing has been removed from it. What clothing did you have in there that you were bringing along for this trip with your father?"

Patrick listed items: a T-shirt and a stocking cap. "We got the jackets from my sisters," he added. "No medical supplies were included."

"In that bag you also had this .45 semiautomatic pistol. Is that correct?"

"Yes, sir."

"And it was fully loaded?"

"Yes, sir."

Burchard proceeded to itemize every object in the gym bag, including a holster for the .45 and clips attached to an ammunition belt. When asked how many rounds were attached to the belt, Patrick said, "Probably forty rounds." Regarding the .22 pistol, Patrick said the gun was in the bag, fully loaded with eight rounds, prior to the shoot-out.

"And did you have an Interdynamics KG-99 also in the bag?"

"Yes, sir."

Burchard also asked about a flare gun. "Was it placed in the bag?"

While Patrick did not recall taking the flare gun from his father's house and placing it in the trunk, he did acknowledge taking the flare gun from the trunk and placing it in the gym bag. Patrick could not explain where the second flare gun, found behind the chicken coop, came from.

Burchard mockingly summarized, "You don't know where the other flare gun came from, and your testimony to this jury is that you brought a flare gun along for search and rescue purposes in case your father had a problem—a medical problem in the mountains?"

"Yes, sir."

"So he's trying to get away from the police, the police are going to kill him, and if he has a medical problem, you just happen to have a flare gun with you so you can shoot it up in the air and get the rescue squad to come and help him. That was your thinking that night?"

"His welfare was my important thought."

Burchard asked about the other items in the gym bag: flares, a knife, and mace. Patrick agreed that they also had been in the bag.

"And the nunchuck sticks?"

"Yes, sir."

"And you were concerned for your father. You wanted to help him through the rough terrain, so you brought all this stuff along just so you could have that T-shirt and that hat with you—what, in case it got cold?" the prosecutor asked cynically.

"I usually take my firearms with me so I know where they are," Patrick said.

"So, you were bringing them through the woods that night in order to keep them safe?"

"When we left the car we were concerned about the girls. If we left the bag in the car, my father's concern was that there might be some problem that might come up leaving the bag in Lila's trunk. So I took the bag with me. That is my usual procedure, sir."

"Didn't you hear your father say, 'I'd rather die than go back to jail'?"

"I don't recall hearing that, sir."

"You don't remember that stuff? Wasn't there a link between the guns and that statement? Didn't your father and you decide to bring the guns along in case you ran into the police?"

"No, sir."

"And right then when you left the car, didn't you and your father decide that if you saw any police you were going to have a shoot-out with them?"

"No, sir. We were trying to avoid any contact with the police."

"I understand you were trying to avoid contact, but you had decided that if you saw them, there was going to be a shootout."

"We had decided nothing like that, sir."

"You put your gym bag in the trunk on the twenty-fifth. When you were told that your father had been arrested, you and your sisters drove to Nespelem, and you put the gym bag in the trunk when you were leaving?"

"Yes, sir."

"And your testimony is that you always travel that way, even to go, what, the ten or twelve miles, maybe fifteen, from Keller to Nespelem?"

"Sometimes, yes, sir."

"To go find out why your father's been arrested, what's going on—on an occasion like that, you still find it necessary to bring this collection of guns, including the 9-millimeter, with you?"

"I did not know when we left Keller whether my father had been arrested or what."

"What, you were bringing the guns so they would be safe?"

"Yes, sir. There are usually a bunch of children at my sister's residence, and rather than leave the bag unattended, I take it with me. That was my usual procedure."

"You mentioned your Interdynamics KG-99 in your testimony. You haven't seen it in evidence here?"

"No, I haven't, sir."

"Where is it, Pat?"

"I don't know, sir. I wish I did."

"You wish you knew where it was?"

"Yes. I wish it were here. I believe it would help us."

"It just disappeared, as far as you know?"

"As far as I know, the last time I saw it was when we were going up the hill. My father fell down, and I picked him up. I was unaware of anything other than him; he was wounded and we were trying to get out of the area, trying to find a safe place. We were scared. He was hurt."

"If we could go back, before you went up the hill, to the time the shooting started, you're behind the chicken coop with your father, right?"

"Yes, sir."

"What weapons did you take from the gym bag?"

"I had the holster belt in one hand and the twenty-two in the other hand, sir."

"And the forty-five was in the holster?"

"Yes, sir."

The prosecutor pointed to a diagram of buildings at the McGinnis residence. "And you were over here by the southwest corner of the chicken coop?"

"Yes, sir."

"And you were trying to hide there to see who was coming up the driveway?"

"To find out who was coming up the driveway is what was going on," Patrick said.

"Well, when you were going to the chicken coop, didn't you see lights from a car on the other side of the property and think that was unusual?"

"Yes, sir, I did."

"And then when you got behind the chicken coop there were more lights?"

"Sometime after that, yes."

"And they were lighting up the side of the hill behind you?"

"Some of it, yes."

"Well, just what did you think, Mr. Hoffman? What was going through your mind right then? These might be trespassers—is that what you were thinking?"

"First we thought it might be the girls coming back, but when they—when the car stopped in the driveway, we went back behind the chicken coop. We had been trying to avoid any contact all evening, and we continued to do so."

"Well, you knew it was the police, didn't you, Mr. Hoffman?"

"How was I to know that, sir?"

"Who would be pulling into your place with all those cars and lights in the middle of the night?"

"I don't know, sir."

"Weren't you running from the police?"

"When we got out of the car?"

"Yeah. Didn't you go overland in order to avoid the police?" asked the prosecutor.

"That was six hours or more, sir."

"Isn't it true, Mr. Hoffman, that before you went to your father's house, you went up on the hill to check the area, to see if any police were parked around there? That's why you were on the hill."

"We were there because my father had a difficult time making the last hill."

"Your father might have had a difficult time, but you were also looking to see if there were any police in the area?"

"That's possible. Yes, sir."

"And when you saw that there weren't any, you decided to cross the road and get onto the property without getting caught?"

"Yes, sir."

"You assumed the police had all gone home. You didn't know that they'd left the property under surveillance."

"This is true."

"When the cars and lights started appearing, you knew it was the police because it couldn't be anybody else, could it?"

"How could I assume that, sir?"

"Okay. Well, did you think it was some friends coming over?"

"No, sir, I did not."

"Did you think it was some burglars coming to break into the house, steal something?"

"I did not know who it was, sir."

"You saw the big lights moving on the hill behind you. What agencies in Nespelem have those kinds of lights?"

"I don't know, sir. I live in Keller."

"You know that police have spotlights, don't you?"

"I suppose so."

"Did you try to look at the cars?"

"No, sir, we were trying to avoid contact with anyone until we found out who was in the driveway. We were trying to avoid any confrontation. Showing ourselves would not have avoided confrontation, sir."

"You were in the dark, weren't you?"

"Yes, sir."

"Plenty of cover back there?"

"Yes, sir."

"And your testimony is that you just didn't look at the vehicles?"

"This is true, sir."

"When you were behind the chicken coop, you had the forty-five and the twenty-two. That's your testimony?"

"Yes, sir."

"And you fired both of them. Is that your testimony?"

"Yes, sir."

"Is your testimony that your father fired a gun or didn't fire a gun?"

"I don't know, sir."

"You don't know?"

"To the best of my recollection, I do not know, sir."

"Isn't it true that your father fired a gun? I'm not talking about the flare gun. You've already said that he fired the flare gun. I'm talking about another gun."

"I cannot say that for certain, sir. I do not know."

"Jeff Epperson—he had been a friend of yours for several years?"

"Yes, sir."

"And you trusted him?"

"Yes, sir."

"He tried to help you?"

"Yes, sir."

"You listened to what he had to say?"

"Yes, sir."

"Did you tell him your father had—"

"Your Honor—" Gardener interrupted.

"—the 9-millimeter gun?" Burchard finished.

Gardner persisted. "This line of questioning must be halted. I request that the jury be removed." At the sidebar he reminded the judge, "The court has ruled on the Epperson testimony. None of this testimony regarding Mr. McGinnis's firing any weapon may be allowed."

The crowd's chatter grew louder as the attorneys sparred, amplified by the high ceilings and large windows of the century-old courthouse. Outside traffic added to the din. Burchard complained, "I still can't hear you, Bud. I guess it's the car out there. I'm sorry, I can't hear you."

"Jack, maybe if you'd calm down, you could hear," Gardner said.

Judge Alumbaugh also was having difficulty. "Order! Order! Let's have order." Observers in the packed courtroom slowly turned their noisy comments down to whispers.

Gardner repeated his protest that none of this testimony regarding Epperson's statements should be allowed. Court rules, specifically the Bruton rule, stipulated that defendants tried jointly may not testify against each other.

Burchard argued that the Bruton rule was no longer in effect. "Mr. McGinnis now has the opportunity to cross-examine the witness against him. The Bruton rule applies only if neither defendant were to testify—that a defendant could implicate a co-defendant and not take the stand."

Gardner protested, "This is precisely the reason we had made our motion for severance."

"I concur with the state that the Bruton rule is no longer in effect," ruled the judge. "The witness may answer the question."

The jury was called back. Mr. Burchard asked Patrick, "Isn't it true that your father did have that 9-millimeter gun?"

"I don't know that for sure, sir."

"Isn't it true that on August twenty-eighth, 1986, in Keller, Washington, you told your friend, Mr. Epperson, that your father had the 9-millimeter gun?"

"That statement to Mr. Epperson could possibly be true. I don't know."

"Isn't that what you told Mr. Epperson?"

"To the best of my recollection, yes."

"Okay. Did you make that up at the time?"

"No, sir."

"Didn't you tell—did your father fire the 9-millimeter gun?"

"Sir, I can't be sure whether or not he did."

"Didn't you tell Mr. Epperson that your father fired the gun?"

"That was an observation from what I saw that night, but I cannot be sure of it."

"From what you saw that night it looked like your father fired the gun, but you couldn't be sure of that?"

"I saw his silhouette; I saw flashes in front of him; I cannot tell for sure whether his finger was pulling a trigger or not, sir."

"You told Mr. Epperson that your father fired the gun?"

"That was my general impression from what I had seen. That was what I was describing to him, about the same space that you are questioning me about now. I was answering the same questions from two people, sir. There was a lot of misquoting, misunderstanding and stuff. I was answering to the best of my knowledge then as I am now, sir."

"Weren't they trying to help?"

"Yes, sir, but there was information that they wanted to know, too."

"Uh huh. And, what? You just didn't think the question of whether your father had fired a gun or not was that important, so maybe you said the wrong thing about it?"

"The most important thing was to know that my father was alive, and that there were problems."

"Okay, and you learned he was in the hospital?"

"I didn't know where he was at that time."

"Didn't Mr. Epperson tell you that they'd taken your father to a hospital in Spokane—medevaced him over there?"

"He just told me that he was alive."

"Your testimony is that when you said 'Good deal,' what you meant was, 'Good deal, my dad's alive,' not 'Good deal, Louis Millard's dead.'"

"That was my feeling, sir."

"Then when Mr. Epperson told you that your father was alive, why didn't you say 'Good deal' then instead of waiting till sometime later when he said that Louis Millard was dead? Why did you wait till he talked about Louis Millard to say that?"

"He said that my father was alive in one statement. I was reading the paper when he told me that there was a police officer dead. It was in answer to the statement that my father was alive."

"You don't recall the conversation between those two statements?"

"There was a lot of conversation going on, sir."

"Mr. Epperson just must be mistaken?"

"I don't know, sir."

"Now, that Interdynamics KG-99, you had two magazines for that?"

"Yes, sir, I did."

"Did you have them taped together end to end?"

"Yes, sir, I did."

"And that was so, when you fired up one magazine, you could pull it out and reload it real fast?"

"It was easier to shoot the weapon in that fashion."

"And you could use that for a hand grip, too—the magazine?"

"Yes, you could."

"How many rounds did you have loaded in it that night?"

"I don't recall for sure."

"Forty, fifty?"

"Forty."

"Okay. And did you take it out of the bag and give it to your father, or did he take it out himself?"

"I don't recall, sir. There was a lot going on in a short amount of time."

"And your testimony is that when you were helping your father up the hill, you just dropped it. It fell out, your father dropped it, or somehow you forgot about it?"

"I had my father on my back. I was trying to get up the hill to get away from the area because there were shots fired. We were in a very tense situation. I was scared. I was trying to find a place to get my father to safety. I was seeking aid, and there was no aid coming to us."

"So your testimony is that the 9-millimeter fell on the ground?"

"That's the only possible time that I know it could have been lost."

"You don't remember having that gun with you when you left your father, assuming that he was dying?"

"I had no weapons when I left my father, sir."

"Okay. So you didn't carry the weapon with you up the hill from your father's location further south?"

"Not to my knowledge, sir. I had my father on my back and I was struggling up a hill, a steep hill."

"Okay. And you're saying that the gun just dropped? You didn't hide the gun?"

"No, sir."

"Well, isn't it true that you took that gun up the hill with you and hid it?"

"No, sir."

"You hid it real good so no one would ever find it?"

"No, sir."

"And the reason you hid it is because you knew a police officer had been shot with it, and you had it in your hand when it happened, and you're blaming your father now?"

"No, sir, that is not true."

"So what? Do you have a theory about this? What? The police found it and got rid of it? What's your theory?"

Price objected to the form of the question, which called for speculation. The objection was sustained.

"Do you remember telling Mr. Epperson that you dropped the gun after you left your father because it was too heavy and you didn't want to carry it?"

"No sir, that's not what I said."

"Isn't it true that you checked the 9-millimeter gun and it had jammed?"

"No, sir."

"That didn't have anything to do with getting rid of it?"

"No, sir."

Price again objected. "The question assumes that he got rid of it, when in fact he has testified differently."

"It doesn't assume it, Your Honor, it challenges his answer," Burchard said.

Price protested, "Your Honor, this is the kind of thing I'm objecting to, is counsel trying to over-prosecute."

Judge Alumbaugh sustained the objection and asked for another direction.

"Now, when you fired a flare, how did that work? When the flare was coming down, your father would shoot, or you would put the gun down and shoot when the area was illuminated. How did that work?"

Price objected again, saying the prosecutor was trying to put his theory of the case in through the mouth of this witness.

The judge asked the prosecutor to limit his question and proceed.

"You fired a flare up, and then what? Your father fired the gun, or you had the gun in the other hand and fired it when the flare was coming down. Which one?"

"In some order like that, sir."

"Okay. And then sometimes your father fired the flare and you fired the gun?"

"Yes."

"As the flares came down, the yard was illuminated, right? It would get bright?"

"Some part of the yard, yes, sir."

"And you could see two officers on the ground, and when they were illuminated you and your father tried to shoot them again?"

"I could see no one, sir. All I could see were muzzle flashes, and I fired back at the muzzle flashes, sir."

"Where were you when you were firing at the muzzle flashes?"

"At the southeast corner of the chicken coop, sir. That's the only place I fired a weapon other than the twenty-two at the top of the—at the middle of the building when the shooting first broke out."

"So you were located at the middle of the building when you fired a weapon?"

"No, sir. I was at the west end of the coop when I heard a shot."

"Did the police fire flares? Didn't you tell Mr. Epperson that that's how this got started—the police fired a flare at you?"

"I don't know, sir. There were flares going up. There were shots going off in a very short time. I was scared. My father was hurt."

"Real simple question, Mr. Hoffman. Two flare guns here, one in your father's hand, one in yours. Were the flares coming out of these flare guns or somebody else's?"

"There were flares…"

Price interrupted, "Excuse me, Mr. Hoffman. Your Honor, he's answered the question. He shot some flares. He said he didn't know if the police were shooting flares. And I think he's answered the question. It's asking him to speculate on what the police were doing, and he said he couldn't tell, didn't even know they were police out there. So what other people were doing, and whether they were shooting flares, this witness is not in a position to know."

The judge asked Mr. Burchard to rephrase his question.

"Mr. Hoffman, were the flares coming out of these two guns or some other guns, some other location?"

"There were flares coming out of our guns. Yes, sir."

"Didn't you tell Mr. Epperson that flares were fired at you first?"

"If I made that statement to Mr. Epperson, yes, I guess it's true."

"Didn't you tell Mr. Epperson that the police fired flares at you first because you wanted to make it look like you'd been attacked by the police?"

"Absolutely not, sir."

"That was a complete lie you told to Mr. Epperson, wasn't it?"

"No, sir."

"And you did it to avoid responsibility for what happened?"

"No, sir."

"And that's not the reason the KG-99 isn't here?"

"I lost it. I don't know where it's at, sir."

"Did you know Louis A. Millard?"

"Yes, sir."

"Did you know he was a tribal police officer?"

"Yes, sir."

"Were you familiar with his voice?"

"Yes, sir."

"You said you emptied the forty-five?"

"At one point, sir, yes."

"How many shots is that?"

"Seven."

"You emptied it, and then didn't you reload it?"

"I guess so."

"Took out another clip, put it in there?"

"I guess so, sir."

"You guess so or is that what you did?"

"Sir, they were still shooting at us at the time. I was trying to repel whoever was shooting at us. I had no choice but to reload and return fire at the muzzle flashes. My father was down, he was bleeding. He could have been dying right there, as far as I knew."

"I know that's what you say, Mr. Hoffman. You said you saw your father fire a gun, or you assume he did. You're not sure, but you saw his silhouette, and saw him fire a gun?"

"That is true, sir."

"Wasn't that the first shot fired that night, your father firing a gun?"

"I cannot be sure of that, sir."

"It might have been?"

"I don't know."

Burchard paused, looked at his notes, and fumbled through the pages. He paused again for some time and then asked about Patrick's appearance on the night of the twenty-sixth. The defendant admitted that he had a beard at the time and considerably longer hair. There was another pause and delay, prompting the judge to ask, "Mr. Burchard, do you have any additional questions?"

"I'm sorry, Your Honor, I was trying to go through my notes and…" After a brief interlude, Burchard regained his focus. "Isn't it true that your father got out of the car at Armstrong Meadows because he simply did not want to go to jail?"

Price objected. "The question is repetitious. The same question was asked an hour and a half ago."

Burchard disagreed. "I want to determine if the threat of going to jail was ever discussed during that time."

Judge Alumbaugh said she would allow a few questions in that area.

The prosecutor continued, "Did your father want out of the car to avoid going to jail?"

"I never talked about the matter with my father."

Burchard continued with questions about McGinnis's locked house and who might have had the keys.

Judge Alumbaugh turned to the prosecutor and said, "It is four thirty. Do you have any additional questions, Mr. Burchard?"

"I'm sorry, Your Honor, I do," Burchard said. "When you saw the flash-lights—did you see flashlights approaching the chicken coop?"

"No, I did not, sir."

"Isn't it true that you were firing at flashlights?"

"No, sir."

"That's all I have, Your Honor."

Chapter 26

Closing Arguments and Verdict

The defense was expected to call for a site visit to confirm their placement of the cage and flags, and offer their video to the jury, but that did not happen. Without warning, Price motioned to rest the defense's case for Patrick Hoffman. Gardner concurred; he did not have any additional witnesses and also was prepared to rest the defense's case for Elmer McGinnis.

Burchard was caught completely off guard. "I was hoping to have the opportunity to ask a few additional questions of Mr. Hoffman—that's number one," he replied. "Number two, I wanted law officials to tour the McGinnis property to see where the boxes and Sergeant Millard's flashlight were located."

"I object to any further examination of Mr. Hoffman. It appeared to me that Mr. Burchard ended his examination. He spent the last half hour with very few questions," Price said.

"Well, the state told the court that it had no additional questions yesterday afternoon. So unless there are other questions on direct, the state is precluded from asking any additional questions," announced the judge.

"I apologize for the structure of my cross-examination of Mr. Hoffman," Burchard confessed to the judge. "I had a hard time going through my notes and asking the questions, and I missed a couple of things." Later, after the trial, Gardner commented that Burchard had been on a roll and then seemed to lose his way toward the end of the day.

While the judge appreciated Burchard's admission, it did not alter her opinion that the state had terminated Hoffman's cross-examination. Judge Alumbaugh also said that she would not entertain further rebuttal testimony concerning Mr. Hoffman's outstanding arrest warrant.

As slowly as the trial had progressed at times, attorneys, the judge, and perhaps the witnesses were all ready for the case to be handed to the jury. The contentious battle over jury instructions had yet to be completely settled. These instructions offered legal guidelines as to how jurors were to evaluate evidence. One proposed instruction defined lawful behavior of police who attempted to make the arrest the morning of August 27. Another dealt with accomplice liability; jurors were instructed to consider whether the words or deeds of both defendants had led to crimes, in this case the murder and assault of tribal police officers. Aiding and abetting crimes before, during, and after the alleged incidents could in effect unburden the state from proving beyond a reasonable doubt who actually killed Officer Millard or wounded Officer Dick.

The aggravated charge was brought because a police officer had been killed. The Washington statute for aggravated first-degree murder included language intended to protect public servants like police. Deadly force that resulted in the death or injury of police performing their duty was considered an aggravated act and was subject to the most extreme sentences.

※ ※ ※

Perhaps due to the prospect of lengthy sessions to finalize jury instructions, the judge adjourned the jury early on Friday, March 27. The judge, attorneys, and defendants also discussed possible dates for the case to be handed to the jury. Elmer suggested Monday morning—he told the judge he wanted to bring the trial to an end as soon as possible. Others suggested an even earlier date: Sunday morning. The judge researched the question of holding court on Sunday and found no legal reason to exclude the weekend.

The sentiment was clear. Everyone was ready to bring the exhausting trial to an end. The judge reminded attorneys that their closings would not be measured in days. "It will be in terms of hours." She anticipated that closing arguments would be lengthy given the many disputed points of law and the number of witnesses. The state had called forty-four witnesses, and the defense had called twenty-two. The judged scheduled closing remarks for Monday with the goal of handing the case to the jury on the same day.

Thirty jury instructions were painstakingly finalized in the confines of the judge's chambers, where attorneys could spread out their papers and approach the task more amicably. Instructions dealt largely with legal definitions; two dealt with police actions; one specified that Elmer's arrest at the council agency on August 25 was legal; another stated, "The entry by police officers onto the McGinnis property at about 2:15 a.m. on August 27, 1986, was lawful."

Both sides spent the weekend preparing closing arguments. The trial began on time Monday morning. The prosecutor had the first and last word.

Burchard stepped toward the jury and explained that criminal intent had been formed early on. The chain of events started with a struggle in the council office, continued with an escape from custody at the hospital, and finished when Elmer and Patrick prepared to do battle with tribal police. The prosecutor then summarized the shoot-out. It started when the defendants shot John Dick in the back. Patrick Hoffman fired the KG-99 atop a chicken cage, killing Lou Millard. He argued that defendants fully intended to kill police officers, given the firing of flares and bullets after the officers were down.

Bud Gardner made a ninety-minute plea to jurors to consider that the bizarre conduct of tribal police had provoked the gunfight. "Police were geared up for a fight, anticipating, perhaps itching, for a confrontation. With bright lights directed to the property, never once did police announce themselves. Such improper police procedures led to a violent confrontation that early morning," Gardner said.

"Mr. McGinnis honestly thought he was going to be killed because he knew too much about the supposed corruption of the governing business council. The shoot-out was a tragedy. There is no question about that. All of this could have been avoided if police had followed Chief Smiskin's order to retire for the night and return with an arrest warrant the next morning."

Gardner, who'd had some bruising encounters with Elmer over defense strategies, made the case for self-defense in his final remarks. McGinnis had little choice but to defend himself against an overwhelming police presence. No mention was made of the validity of Elmer's corruption charges.

During a pause while Gardner reviewed his notes, the judge asked, "How much longer will you need to complete your closing argument?"

"I have a few more statements," Gardner replied. He closed the ninety minutes, saying, "There was never a coordinated plan where each officer knew what his responsibility was, or even an ongoing assessment of officers' locations during the early morning incursion onto the residence. It is clear that police were complicit in this tragic incident."

Price took his turn. He started his closing with an attack on a major premise of the prosecution's case. "I said it was an unsolved shooting during my opening…and it still is. After all the testimony, there is still no proof that Patrick Hoffman shot Mr. Millard. All we know is, Louis Millard was hit in the dark, and we don't know by whom.

"The police were to blame for provoking the fight," he told the jury. "They were primed; they were mad because McGinnis had been an annoyance to them." Price pulled no punches with the jury. He placed most of the blame for the "maddening tragedy" on Officer Dick. "John Dick said he felt responsible for Millard's death. He knew he fouled up so badly that a shooting happened and a death occurred," Price said firmly. "John Dick left police work because he felt so badly for what he had done."

Price repeated John Dick's testimony that he felt a bee sting sensation under his left arm and began to fall forward. "Consider his testimony. Dick yelled that he was wounded, then said he heard Millard say, 'John, if you're hit, get down.' It was illogical for Dick to be standing at that point. Lou Millard said those words fearing that he had hit Dick, and it was best for him to remove himself from the line of fire."

"As to the charge of first-degree murder, the defendants were tried for the wrong crime. First-degree murder would require that the defendants intended to kill Millard specifically," he challenged. "How could they have done that not knowing who was on the property?"

Price attacked prosecutors for conducting an unfair trial. He accused them of not wanting to present all the evidence for fear of a not-guilty verdict. He suggested that Sergeant Carden lied when he said he didn't fire his gun. "An FBI lab check of police weapons did not occur until months after the shooting incident. The bottom line is, there was no incontrovertible evidence that proved where the bullet came from that killed Louis Millard.

"Elmer and Patrick tried to avoid a confrontation," Price stated. "By the time the flares were fired, Officer Millard had already been hit. Five police officers said they couldn't see Millard, yet somehow McGinnis and Hoffman knew he was there to shoot."

Burchard began his nearly two-hour closing statement acknowledging that the jury faced a tough decision. "A good deal of the state's evidence is circumstantial, and the gun responsible for Lou Millard's death has not been found. Although it was not proven which man shot which officer, an accomplice is guilty, just as guilty, as the principal.

"As the officers came up to the chicken coop, did the defendants deliberate at that point? When officers shined the flashlight behind the chicken coop, did they deliberate? When they raised the gun and pointed at the officer's back, did they deliberate? When they pointed the gun at Louis Millard and pulled the trigger, did they deliberate? That's what 'premeditated' means," Burchard said. "And as to the death of Louis Millard, that's what we have to prove: that they thought about it. Whoever pulled the trigger thought about it beforehand for more than a moment. Minutes, hours, days, weeks—all that satisfies the proof as long as it's more than a moment in time, as long as there is some reflection before the trigger is pulled," the prosecutor emphasized.

"And that's not as complicated as it sounds when you stop and think about it, because isn't that what the proof is? And isn't that reasonably evaluating the evidence, how the defendants acted in this particular situation?"

Turning from his somewhat temperate summary of the legal arguments for conviction, the prosecutor went on the attack. "The defendants fired first, shooting John Dick in the back and killing Lou Millard with the 9-millimeter semiautomatic pistol. The evidence is clear. The casings found behind the chicken coop matched the bullet extracted from Sergeant Millard. Patrick Hoffman admitted to having the KG-99 in his gym bag, and ultimately disposing of the gun when he fled the scene."

To dramatize for the jury his version of the deadly shooting, the prosecutor held up enlarged photos of Lou Millard's body facedown and faceup on the ground, along with a photo of a semiautomatic KG-99 assault pistol. The prosecutor picked up one of the firearms introduced as evidence and took aim at an imaginary subject. "Hoffman held the gun in such a position, and took careful, steady aim as the officers approached, and then deliberately fired the gun with the intent of killing the police officers," he said slowly.

"The defendants killed Louis Millard with that KG-99, and the evidence is right here," Burchard declared while pointing to the casings, the bullet, and a photo of the gun. "Twenty-five times these men put their fingers on triggers and shot at police officers." Pointing at Patrick and Elmer, Burchard argued that the ferocity of their attacks proved they were not involved in an accidental shooting or a case of mistaken identity.

"Now, what happened to this gun is that Hoffman knew a police officer had been shot with it, and he took it up in the hills and got rid of it. He hid it so nobody would ever find it."

Burchard quoted Patrick's reply to Price's inquiry about the location of the gun. "'I don't know, sir. As far as I know, the last time I saw it was when we were going up the hill.' Did Patrick really not know where the gun was? Look at what Patrick said to Jeff Epperson after the shootings. He told Epperson he had disposed of the gun. Epperson testified about his conversation with

Patrick on their way to the Okanogan Sheriff's Office. He said he got rid of it, or more or less stashed it on the way up the hill so he wouldn't have to pack it. It was getting too heavy to pack himself."

At last, the grueling and combative case was handed to the jury on March 31, 1987. The lengthy trial extended from October to early spring for a total of approximately six months.

Jurors faced the daunting task of unraveling some reasonable sequence of events, starting with Elmer confronting the Fergusons to settle a debt over a motorcycle, to the aftermath of a shoot-out where one officer was killed and another wounded.

A minority of vocal supporters of the defendants felt adamant justice was not being served. Some, like Sony George, saw the trial as a sham, a kangaroo court jumping from one venue to another to nail Elmer and Pat for good. Both were attacked for what they knew about corrupt officials, just like Bobby Jo Covington.

News coverage spread beyond Okanogan County to urban media markets on both sides of the state. Media contamination was a major concern. Judge Alumbaugh agreed with attorneys on this and chose to sequester the jury.

One of the fourteen jurors had already been excused due to illness. County Clerk Jackie Bradley drew one name from a jar, and one other juror was excused to finalize the twelve-member panel. The judge instructed both jurors not to discuss the case with anyone until the jury had reached a decision.

Late afternoon on Monday, March 31, Judge Alumbaugh reviewed instructions to the jury. Jurors were told that if they could not reach a verdict by the end of the day, they would be sequestered at the Cedars Inn Motel about a mile from the courthouse.

The jury retreated to a small jury room in the historic Okanogan Courthouse and deliberated late into the evening with no verdict. They retired to the motel and returned the next day, April 1. Two questions emerged during their deliberations, one early in the morning and the other around noon. The jury foreman, David Dubrouillet, submitted the jury's first question. "Is the KREM videotape of Jeff Burnside's interview with Elmer McGinnis evidence?"

The judge replied in writing, "The videotape of Elmer McGinnis is evidence."

The jury's second question was more controversial. "Does the absence of premeditation for one defendant make them not an accomplice as defined in instruction number seven?"

The judge and attorneys reviewed their options as to a response. Price argued that the judge should answer in the affirmative. "There was no evidence that Patrick Hoffman had plotted, discussed, or in any way mentioned premeditated intent to kill Louis Millard or John Dick."

Burchard countered, "The answer is clearly no. The evidence did show intent to do battle with police."

Listening to the arguments, Judge Alumbaugh concluded, "It is up to the jury to apply the instructions as they understand them." The judge wrote out her reply for the jury to read. "To answer your question, please read the instructions again as a whole."

After deliberating for a total of thirteen hours, the jury verdict was delivered at 8:23 p.m. About a dozen spectators and eight officers were in attendance. Most observers had left. Families and supporters of Lou Millard had gone home. Likewise, Elmer and Patrick's family were absent.

Elmer McGinnis could hardly control his tremor as the jury foreman stood to offer the verdict. The bailiff relayed the jury's verdict to the judge. The judge scanned the jury forms and arranged them in order. Defendants were asked to stand as the judge read the verdict.

"We the jury find the defendant Elmer McGinnis guilty of the crime of murder in the first degree as charged. In regard to the special interrogatory, has the state proven beyond a reasonable doubt that defendant McGinnis knew or reasonably should have known that Louis A. Millard was a law enforcement officer who was performing his official duties at the time of the killing? The jury response is yes.

"We the jury find the defendant Patrick Gene Hoffman guilty of the crime of murder in the first degree as charged. In regard to the special interrogatory, has the state proven beyond a reasonable doubt that defendant Hoffman knew or reasonably should have known that Louis A. Millard was a law enforcement officer who was performing his official duties at the time of the killing? The jury response is yes."

The defendants' fate was sealed. Patrick Hoffman's eyes swelled with tears, and Elmer McGinnis stood trembling and shaking his head.

The defendants were also found guilty of aggravated first-degree assault.

Judge Alumbaugh excused the jurors, advising them that they were free to speak to others about the trial, but there was no obligation to do so. She warned jurors not to say anything to anyone that they would not later be willing to repeat under oath.

Craig Brown of the *Wenatchee World* reported that the courtroom atmosphere was quite somber. Burchard showed no signs of elation. "All I have to say is, I'm tired, and I'm very proud of the police around here and the jury." Burchard shook the hand of each juror as they were excused.

Chapter 27

Appeals

Elmer and Patrick were handcuffed. Responding to a reporter's question about what would happen next, Gardner said it was fairly certain that a motion to set aside the verdict would be made.

Chief Smiskin told the press, "Needless to say, we're pleased with the outcome." He cited the "fantastic job" done by Prosecutors Burchard and Hicks. Smiskin was far less generous with the defense attorneys. "I think they discredited John Dick needlessly. Their accusations of tribal corruption were asinine."

The hearing for appeals motions was set for April 7 and sentencing on April 14. Gardner arrived at the appeals hearing unsure of whether he should proceed. His relationship with Elmer had deteriorated. A young but seasoned attorney, Gardner was quite personable and respected in the legal community. But his personality was not on trial. For Elmer, his attorney had failed to expose corrupt witnesses who were paid off to testify against him.

Dr. Cressey's testimony vindicated for Elmer that the wrong defense had been offered. The reputable forensic psychiatrist had testified the defendant was not psychotic and did not meet standards for insanity at the time of the incident. Elmer was critical of his attorney calling Dr. Cressey to the stand in the first place. Why, he asked, was his mental status questioned rather than calling more witnesses to expose tribal corruption?

Reflecting on recent contacts with Elmer, Gardner stood before the judge and said, "I should advise the court that my client has directed me not to speak on his behalf at this proceeding."

Hearing this, Elmer begrudgingly announced, "Go ahead."

Gardner looked back at his client. "Go ahead?"

Elmer nodded.

"Okay." Gardner recited familiar defense arguments on his "arrest of judgment" petition. Their defenses were such that each defendant required separate trials. Gardner called prosecutor conduct into question. "There was also an irregularity in proceedings," he said, referring to the defense's problem with timely procurement of state evidence. Improper remarks were made during the trial and closing. Jury selection was tainted due to pretrial and trial publicity. The presence of high-security measures in the courtroom had a prejudicial effect, suggesting that the clients were potentially violent. The participation of a special deputy prosecutor during pretrial and the participation of federal officials throughout the trial had a cumulative effect that well could have convinced the jury that a guilty verdict was necessary. In summary, the state failed to provide sufficient evidence to allow a reasonable trier of fact to find beyond a reasonable doubt that the defendants were guilty of the crimes charged.

Seeing the large number of appeal issues in both defense motions, Burchard hardly wanted to add one more to the list: lack of representation for defendant McGinnis. "Your Honor, could I ask the court to inquire into one area just for the record? I just—I wasn't sure whether Mr. Gardner has the authority to speak for Mr. McGinnis at this hearing today or not."

"I don't know if it's clear, Your Honor," replied Gardner. "I've been told on three previous occasions that Mr. McGinnis did not desire to continue my services. As I stood up to say that to the court, Mr. McGinnis touched my arm and told me to go ahead."

Judge Alumbaugh directed her question to Elmer. "Are you objecting to Mr. Gardner speaking on your behalf, at least for the purposes of this particular hearing?"

"Some things I am, Your Honor. Some things I'm not," Elmer replied. "I'm not objecting for the simple reason that we are not guilty, and our civil rights have been walked all over with muddy feet right from the start, and whereby different law enforcement officers testified and lied right on the witness stand to my knowledge. I've been—"

The judge cut Elmer off. "In regard to Mr. Gardner assisting you in this proceeding—and I will ask you later if you want to make some additional statements—but in regard to his representing you here for these motions, are you willing to allow him to go forward and argue them on your behalf?"

"Right, Your Honor," Elmer answered.

Gardner summarized the remainder of his objections, emphasizing that the tragic event would have not happened had police shown restraint and followed proper police procedure.

Price stepped forward and gave an overview of his thirty-page affidavit arguing for a new trial. The first ten pages specifically addressed misconduct by the prosecutor. Prosecutorial misconduct motions were raised during trial, but in Price's appeal he took the prosecutor's conduct to a higher level. The tone of the appeal and his oral arguments made it clear that he felt professionalism had been breached.

The prosecutor had failed to provide evidence to the defense expert in a timely manner. Evidence favorable to the defense was not available prior to the trial, specifically the 9-millimeter bullet found in the eastern pasture. Price accused the prosecutor of improperly introducing Patrick's pending arrest warrant. The prosecutor had impugned the "motives and intentions" of defense counsel when questioning witnesses.

Price chastised Burchard for his conduct during closing. "He held up one of the firearms as though taking careful aim at the subject, and told the jury that it was his belief that defendant Hoffman had held the gun in such a position, taking careful, steady aim as the officers approached, and then intentionally fired the gun with the intent of killing the police officers." Price argued that this deliberate distortion of evidence on closing was further evidence of prosecutorial misconduct and cumulatively was sufficient grounds to set aside the verdict.

In his oral and written argument, Price attacked the court's handling of the case, citing errors in judgments. He argued two instances: the lesser included instruction issue and the jury's question regarding accomplices and premeditation. Price challenged that the court should have "taken the bull by the horns" and insisted that lesser included instructions be given in spite of the defendants' rejection, noting, "There are Constitutional protections that rise to a much higher standard." While he appreciated the quandary of the court to protect the defense's rights without directing them on this matter, Price said, "The jury was left with little choice but to punish those who were at the scene where Mr. Millard was killed or set the defendants free."

The jury's first vote came out eight to four for Patrick Hoffman's acquittal. Price argued that this vote had taken place before the jury questioned the judge about whether the absence of premeditation by one defendant does not make them an accomplice as defined in instruction number seven. "If the judge had answered in the affirmative to this question, my client would have been acquitted. It's my belief that the jury, wanting justice to be done, swerved from their duty to stick to the essential elements of the crime. They felt it was important that there be punishment, and so they circumvented the element of premeditation," Mr. Price said forcefully.

"There was no evidence offered as to the mental state of my client before or during the shoot-out," Price said. "All we know is that gunfire broke out while both defendants were behind the chicken coop. For the jury to find Mr. Hoffman guilty, they had to determine that he specifically shared the premeditated intent of Mr. McGinnis prior to the shooting, and only then would they be allowed to find Hoffman guilty as an accomplice."

Price criticized the court for not granting separate trials. Clearly there were different defenses, yet the jury did not have the option to consider each independently. "If this trial had been separated, it would have been much quicker," Price posited. "Much of the testimony about hard feelings between

Mr. McGinnis and the tribal council would not have been introduced, nor would that acrimony have been attributed to Patrick Hoffman."

Burchard's rebuttal was brief. He submitted a seventeen-page answer to both post-trial defense motions. He limited his remarks to whether defendants had received a fair trial. He reminded the judge that extensive efforts to hear their defense were evident. The court had provided approximately $150,000 for defense expenses, weeks of pretrial motions (some at first blush having questionable merit), and then six weeks of trial.

"The jury sat and listened to the law and the evidence, and found unanimously that both defendants were guilty of both charges. This is a jury, from what I can see, that had no doubt of any kind. Now, after all this, the defendants are still calling foul, expressing no remorse, no sorrow, no nothing except themselves," Burchard said stridently. "I talked to seven of the jurors, and I can tell the court that the ones that I talked to are angry." He went on to explain how these jurors felt that, after six weeks of service, to be attacked by the local paper as being stupid or involved in misconduct was particularly offensive. "These jurors told me that there was no jury misunderstanding, and there was no filling in the blanks with passion or prejudice. The court instructed the jurors as to the elements of the offense as required by law and it was their duty to find them present beyond a reasonable doubt."

As to arguments about premeditation, Burchard said it was due to assumptions or misunderstandings of the defense about the meaning of premeditation as it applied in this case. "These interpretations should not cloud what the evidence is, what the law is, or the conclusions reached."

Burchard noted, "These arguments are contained in my written brief. In summary, the defendants received an extremely fair trial, and the court has not made any reversible error that would require a new trial or an arrest of judgment."

The judge stated, "I have read the briefs and today will respond to only one issue, namely the lesser included instruction query to the jury. Regarding Mr. Price's assertion that the court was in a quandary, I did not see it in that light. The defendants were briefed on the implications of the instruction before the final arguments. I requested that both reconsider their decision with their attorneys over the weekend. The court again reminded both defendants that they were entitled to the lesser included offenses instruction. Both refused."

The judge continued, "As to the motions for arrest of judgment and a new trial, I find that there was sufficiency of proof of all the material elements of the crimes charged for the jury to reach the decision they reached. Both motions are denied."

Sentencing was a pro forma exercise for aggravated murder: a life sentence without the possibility of parole for Elmer Edward McGinnis and Patrick Gene Hoffman. On the matter of the first-degree assault charge for both defendants, there was some discretion. Burchard, who earlier chastised the defendants for their lack of contriteness, did acknowledge that the state had some reservations about their case. Burchard explained that the prosecution had not sought the death penalty for two reasons. "One, there was no clear proof of who pulled the trigger that killed Officer Millard. Two, a jury would most likely not impose capital punishment in this case."

After sentencing, the defendants were given a chance to address the court.

Chapter 28

Elmer Has His Say

"Mr. McGinnis, would you like to speak to the court?" asked the judge. "Under condition, Your Honor, that I am not interrupted by the so-called prosecution or untarnished law enforcement official, for the simple reason that I believe I have been far more honest and honorable than the ones that I seen that took the witness stand against us," Elmer said.

Elmer had waited for this moment throughout the trial. He rose and stood tall, just as he did when he addressed his neighbors in the Advocates for Colville meetings. "We are not guilty. And if you and others would consider different aspects in the case where the prosecutors did not prove beyond a doubt; and Jack, professing to give sound evidence as if he had been there at the time. Myself, I could not see…nothing, what was going on. I did not know who was on the place. Somebody was on the place prior to me getting there. And I know as sure as God put green apples on a tree that I was the first one shot down. I can show you exactly where the shot came from, where I was at the time, and it never has coincided with any of the prosecutor's wild dreams that he cooked up. Right here, Your Honor. There is one badge there. There is another badge there. I've got another one at home, a US law enforcement. I've put thirteen and a half years in law enforcement and approximately two and a half years of law schooling while I was in service, not counting the schooling I took to qualify ahead of time.

"And my reading over, going over all those police reports, as well as the FBI reports—I went over those three to four dozen times. And if a person goes over, like the so-called FBI officers that tell damn lies in here should have intelligence enough to do, they can pinpoint exactly in those reports who done the killing, who done the shooting. It was not I and my boy. And if you want me to name them, I will name them.

"But one thing's for sure, that bounty that the tribal council put out on me and my boy for digging up document evidence against their illegal doing—fraud, embezzlement, illegal land transactions—that should have been entered as evidence and given to the jury to see. Where big money is involved, any big corporation, they buy at any time anyone to mold things the way they want to cover up. I did not have anything to cover up, neither did my boy, neither do my children.

"But why is it that the council uses the tribal police as a mafia gang, pulls girls out of an auto with drawn, cocked guns to the sides of their heads? What did my daughters do to deserve being treated that way? There's no justice. There's no honest law enforcement, not when they'll get on the stand and lie when the courtroom is supposed to be an honorary place where truth is supposed to be told and upheld. Not no imaginable deal like the prosecutors told like they were right there at the time. Who knows, maybe they were there. I don't know who shot me. I never did see no one.

"Why was my home broken into before all the shooting ended? Why was my home ransacked and documented paper taken out? Why was I shot, and my children's dogs killed needlessly, just for wanton killing, right there inside my home, damaged beyond repair? Then some people call it honesty. I don't."

"Is there anything further you wanted to tell the court, Mr. McGinnis?" the judge asked after a brief pause.

"We're innocent," Elmer concluded.

Patrick deferred from adding anything beyond what his father and Mr. Price had said other than to repeat his father's plea. "We are not guilty, and hope that the court considers that above all else. Thank you."

The remainder of the hearing concerned completing the procedural steps required after a verdict. Judge Alumbaugh requested that a telephone conference be scheduled in two weeks to complete unfinished tasks. Statutory requirements for capital cases required that each defendant have an attorney assigned to him for the automatic appeal. Bud Gardner reiterated that he would not be serving as Elmer McGinnis's attorney, but would work in transition with whoever was appointed for that purpose.

Interestingly, Price made the following comment: "But for a chance meeting many months ago, I probably would never have seen the criminal arena in my practice again. For some reason, God or otherwise, I am involved in this case. I am committed to it and I will remain as counsel." How prophetic were those words. Richard Price's defense of Patrick Hoffman carved significant attorney hours from his active civil practice from December 1986 to the final arguments made in the Washington Supreme Court in January 1991.

Epilogue

On January 10, 1991, after reviewing some eighty issues on appeal in the *State v. Hoffman* case, the majority of justices on the Washington Supreme Court could find no basis for court error in the trial.

Richard Price had persevered for nearly four years, representing Patrick Hoffman at all stages of appeal. His appeal before the state supreme court was exhaustive, arguing objections raised earlier on matters such as jurisdiction, the severance motion, the accomplice liability instruction, and prosecutorial misconduct. Price steadfastly insisted after the verdict that his client had not been given a fair trial and the verdict should be overturned.

More than a decade after the supreme court decision, Justice James Andersen commented to me at a social gathering that on first reading of this case he was skeptical that the trial would be upheld. Upon closer reading, he had never seen so many issues raised where the court affirmed each in favor of the state.

Price had offered to drop out as Patrick Hoffman's appellate lawyer for the Third District Court of Appeals, but Patrick, along with Deputy Clerk Patsy, insisted that Price continue.

Burchard represented the state in all appeals and prevailed for each challenge. After the trial, his tenure as Okanogan County prosecutor proved successful. After serving six years as prosecutor, he opted in 1998 to run for Okanogan Superior Court judge, and won. He went on to serve for nineteen years, retiring in 2012.

Elmer McGinnis never trusted attorneys throughout the trial and thereafter. Elmer insisted that he serve as his own attorney, with attorney Paul Wassen assisting him. He filed briefs quoting statutory and case law, mostly federal law, showing in quasi-bulleted form how his rights had been violated.

Elmer and Patrick were sent to one of the toughest prisons in the Northwest, Washington State Penitentiary at Walla Walla. Elmer's health progressively deteriorated. After serving thirteen years, he was transferred to a secure hospital bed in the Yakima County corrections facility.

Elmer's contact with his family was limited. An exchange of letters with his youngest daughter, Laura, was virtually all the contact he had. Contact with Patrick Hoffman was prohibited, and the two were segregated from each other while serving their sentence in Walla Walla.

Elmer McGinnis passed away on December 29, 2001. He was seventy-nine years old. Fellow native inmates beat their drums, and Indian rituals were carried out as his weak heart finally came to a rest. His last wishes were to be with his family, but no family members were present for his last moments.

Deputy Clerk Patsy and Patrick Hoffman grew closer as the trial progressed. Patrick reflected that the deputy clerk had made friendly overtures throughout the trial. At first he was suspicious that she was working for the prosecutor, but her attention increased until it was clear that she was sympathetic to his defense.

After the verdict, their romance blossomed. Patsy regularly visited Patrick. For his birthday, she baked him a cake. Patrick crafted a bracelet as a gift. Patrick finally proposed, and a quiet marriage ceremony was conducted in the visitor's area of the Walla Walla penitentiary.

Patrick remained in regular contact with Patsy over the years. She retained her position as a deputy clerk, overlapping Burchard's tenure as superior court judge.

Patsy never changed her view on Patrick's innocence. She believed the evidence had been altered by the state to cover up how tribal police had killed Sergeant Millard and seriously wounded Elmer.

It was clear when I interviewed Patsy and Judge Burchard during the summer of 2006 that the Hoffman and McGinnis trial had not been forgotten. Judge Burchard was gracious and gave interesting accounts of the trial and his post-trial impressions. He provided photos and other items connected to the trial for me to briefly examine in an adjacent office.

Patsy also agreed to answer questions about the trial. Among other miscarriages of justice, Patsy accused Burchard of hiding a revolver that police had used in the shoot-out. She claimed that a tribal officer told her that a switch had been made of police revolvers during the initial investigation. She did not offer a name.

Overall, Patsy was cooperative and candid in her assessment of the trial. She strongly criticized the judge for what she saw as biased rulings against the defendants. She was most upset that the judge had taken a call from a law enforcement official regarding the evidence. Again, no name was offered as to the source or content of the call. Judge Alumbaugh did note in her accounts of the trial that she had contacted Sheriff Johnny Johnston over security concerns in the courtroom.

Patrick Hoffman initially declined an interview, but thought it over and had a change of heart. He had been transferred to Monroe Correctional Complex for medical reasons. After an exchange of letters and formalities with officials, Patrick agreed to a taped interview in the summer of 2007.

I was somewhat surprised by the interview location. The assistant warden directed us to a table and chairs in the middle of a large empty room. Patrick entered behind us and approached the table wearing no leg irons or cuffs. I introduced Judi Kehl, who assisted in the interview and later transcribed notes.

Patrick was cordial. Other than the assistant warden, no correctional staff or inmates were present. Patrick was in good shape and looked quite dapper, with neatly trimmed hair and a pressed shirt.

Patrick began the interview by describing his current assignments at Monroe. He was proud of his involvement with other Native Americans, where the peace pipe was shared and rituals enacted. Unexpectedly, he asked if I had any recent contact with Patsy. Patsy apparently had informed him of our previous interview. He went on to say that a year had passed since he'd had any contact with Patsy. He said with apparent remorse their relationship had suffered a setback. After many years traveling, coordinating her schedule to attend appeals, and providing moral support, Patsy had cut off contact—no visits, no replies to his letters. Patrick wanted to send her a message: "My feelings have not waned."

Two decades had passed since the trial. Few family visitors had checked on his status. Serving time as a lifer had not been easy. There was a fight with his cellmate that put him in solitary for a month and diminished his chances of leaving the tough Walla Walla prison.

Patsy had been instrumental in getting the transfer approval to Monroe for medical reasons. Doing time at Monroe was much easier, and he had found his niche with other inmates.

We then discussed the trial. I reminded Patrick that Elmer repeatedly had pressed Dale Kohler over the allotment issue traced back to John McGinnis. Furthermore, I pointed out that Elmer was quite upset that his daughters were not enrolled as Colvilles. Could Patrick give more background as to how the business council had thwarted Elmer? Patrick did not directly respond to any of these observations. Given his silence, I asked Patrick directly, "Had Elmer discussed any of the allotment issues with you?"

Unexpectedly he answered, "I really didn't get to talk to him about that so much. Most of our conversations dealt with corruption in the tribal council. We did talk about the death of Bobby Jo Covington." Almost twenty years later, Patrick insisted that tribal police had shoved the former councilman off the curve of the road while returning home on his motorcycle.

"Was there corruption?" I asked.

Patrick repeated the Mount Tolman gold find as proof of corruption. He complained that this proof was never offered during the trial or brought up on appeal later. Two decades after the trial, Bud Gardner commented in an interview that he could not find documents to support any of these claims.

After exhausting all appeals, the sentence given to both defendants raises a question as to equal justice, specifically for murder convictions in Washington State. Consider that the infamous Green River serial killer, Gary Ridgeway, who was convicted for the murder of forty-nine women, mostly prostitutes, received the same sentence as Patrick Hoffman and Elmer McGinnis. Ridgeway, Elmer, and Hoffman were all sent to Washington State Penitentiary at Walla Walla to serve the same sentence: life without possibility of parole.

Comparing the two cases, wide differences seem apparent as to how courts handled the aggravated first-degree murder charges. In the Gary Ridgeway case, the defendant carried out murders with extreme indifference to life, luring his victims to his pickup and methodically strangling them.

After protests from families who were living with the unsettling suspicion that their loved ones may have been one of Ridgeway's victims, King County Prosecutor Norman Maleng agreed to a plea that reduced Ridgeway's sentence from the death penalty to life without parole if he agreed to identify other victims. Maleng defended the plea bargain by arguing that discovering the truth of what happened in unsolved cases had greater value than carrying out an execution.

Maleng achieved his objective. Gary Ridgeway gave details leading to the remains of many of the forty-nine victims, in addition to some twenty other victims who also may have been his target. While Mr. Maleng's reasoning has merit, how does this precedent square against the sentence for Hoffman and McGinnis, where Burchard admitted during sentencing that there was no clear proof of who pulled the trigger that killed the officer?

Consider another Washington murder case, where prosecutors invoked the aggravated murder statute against Charles Champion, an eighteen-year-old troubled youth. The defendant was charged for the murder in 2001 of Des Moines police officer Steven Underwood. Prosecutors initially sought the death penalty. The officer had stopped to question the youth, who was walking along Pacific Highway with other teens. Champion, who had a record of assault, fired four shots at the officer—one bullet directed at his head.

The death penalty was only averted by the eighteen-year-old defendant after he agreed to plead guilty. Four years later, after delays and a bevy of attorneys representing Champion, the defendant was sentenced to twenty-six to thirty-four years after prosecutors agreed to reduce the charge to first-degree murder. While mitigating factors like Champion's age and background may have weighed in the prosecutors' final decision, Champion's final guilty plea to the murder charge spared him a life sentence without parole.

Given Champion's actions and plea, there was little question as to his intent to do deadly harm. Officer Underwood's status was never in doubt—the officer was in uniform and on active duty carrying out his official duties as a police officer.

Both Elmer and Patrick insisted that they did not know who was intruding on the property, and police never identified themselves. Both defendants steadfastly maintained their innocence. It was on this basis that both defendants opted to try their case with no lesser included instructions to the jury. Had they agreed to the lesser instruction, the verdict could have resulted in a reduced sentence. According to post-verdict interviews, jurors had considered second-degree murder charges even though the instruction had not been given.

Should any defendant be maximally penalized for arguing his or her innocence in cases where police are victimized? By taking a plea agreement, Ridgeway and Champion avoided the death penalty in the former case and a life sentence in the latter. With good time, Charles Champion could be released at age forty-four, while Patrick Hoffman faces the prospect of never being released.

Chief Joseph likely would have understood such injustice. Elmer McGinnis was hardly a traditionalist. To the contrary, Elmer was not unlike other Colville patriots who enlisted for military service during World War II and other wars. He served his country and he believed in the Constitution, in particular the enforcement of laws. Ironically in some sense, the aims of the Dawes Severalty Act had been accomplished. Acculturation was evident.

In spite of their differences, the two Indian advocates seem to merge on the question of sovereignty. Both Chief Joseph and Elmer railed at white exploitation of Indian land and resources. Joseph relentlessly insisted that treaties and laws were broken, as were promises to right these breaches. In the end, the venerated chief and his Wallowa band never returned to their homeland.

≑ ≑ ≑

It was April 1987 after the trial ended. Jo Anne and I returned to Okanogan County for the judge to sign off on final papers for the trial. We returned to the Cariboo Inn in Okanogan to enjoy a perfect omelet again, this time for lunch. The asparagus was not as crisp, but the trimmings of the garlic Texas toast and seasonal fruit were as we remembered. I recall her voicing relief, just as attorneys did during sentencing, that the trial had finally ended. She told me she did not want to talk about local news in Kittitas County.

I obliged. The newspaper accounts of budgetary problems linked to the court continued. Most of the stories swirled around the juvenile office and accrued costs to house juveniles separate from adults. Attorneys continued to boycott the court, save for juvenile trials and a smattering of civil and criminal cases. Of the civil and criminal trials, most were outside attorneys representing local clients.

Jo Anne filed for reelection 1988. Inexorably, or so it seemed at the time, Kittitas County Bar members and county commissioners prevailed. The Kittitas County Bar selected Mike Cooper, an amicable litigator who was not wed to any major law firm, as their preferred candidate. He was judged by his peers to be fair-minded. Opponents of Judge Alumbaugh got behind the new candidate and waged a successful campaign. Cooper's campaign focused on bringing a halt to wasteful court spending and an end to having cases tried by outside judges.

Her brief tenure as a pioneer woman in law serving a rural conservative county came to an end. We migrated to the Fremont neighborhood in Seattle. There, Jo Anne served as a substitute judge, primarily in King County. Building a local reputation, Jo Anne ran for judge in King County in 1992 and won. It was aptly rewarding given her past. She continued her career as judge until she retired in 2002.

While serving in King County, Jo Anne's reputation as a hardworking judge taking on a relatively heavy caseload drew praise from other judges. Her record on appeals, having a minimum number of her cases overturned, affirmed her place on the bench.

A virulent cancer led to her death in May 2003. She was not present to hear Justice Andersen's salutary remarks as to how the judge conducted the trial.

Kittitas County residents did not forget her reform efforts. After her death, citizens gathered at the Kittitas County Courthouse to pay tribute. A memorial plaque was placed in the hallway of the Kittitas Superior Court, recognizing her accomplishments in juvenile reform and forging advocacy programs for youth and adolescents. Judge Mike Cooper was the honorary master of ceremonies for the event. Former Kittitas County Sheriff Bob Barrett, while acknowledging his disagreement with the judge over the treatment of juveniles, recalled that he had great respect for her, as did his officers in the department.

A final memorial for Jo Anne Alumbaugh was held on campus at Central Washington University, where many involved in the grassroots movement for reform in the local judicial system celebrated her life. Her reforms in handling youth and domestic cases set precedents that still remain.

And not to be ignored, Jo Anne pioneered the way for other women to take up law careers in conservative counties. Women engaged in law careers in Kittitas County have nearly reached parity with men. Three women have been elected as judge since her defeat. Her 1984 campaign theme for judge was prescient: "It's Time for a Change."

Acknowledgments

I want to send special thanks to many on and off the Colville reservation who offered their observations and insights of the trial, backgrounds of the defendants, and tribal historical perspectives. Particular praise is offered to Laura McGinnis and her sister Lila for providing their father's legal papers and accounts of events. Their gifts of homemade huckleberry pie and preserves were a special treat. As to the trial, Prosecutor Jack Burchard was quite informative in his perspective of the evidence presented at trial. Similarly, defense attorneys Richard Price and Bud Gardner provided invaluable takes on defense challenges of the case. I am particularly indebted to Richard Price for his review and comments on an earlier draft. My appreciation is extended to Judi Kehl who generously assisted in interviews, and transcribing notes and a taped recording of Patrick Hoffman. Not least among those who made this book possible, I am deeply indebted to my editor Brad Pauquette, who tirelessly did all he could to tighten, correct, and strengthen my prose in earlier drafts. I own fully any and all errors within my account of events, and these are not attributable to any sources for the book.

About the Author

After retirement as a professor of psychology in 2002, Richard Alumbaugh came upon a file box from a murder case heard by his deceased wife, Jo Anne. Subsequent years spent investigating the backgrounds of the accused and the state's evidence left unanswered questions as to the guilt and innocence of the father and son who were Colville enrollees. The author currently enjoys the sunshine of Arizona during colder months, biking and playing tennis, somehow under the delusional impression he is faster and hits the ball more accurately with age.